Winning **On** and **Off** the Court

A Parent's Guide to Creating
World Class Tennis Players and People

Ryan Henry &
Luke Bourgeois

Praise

Congratulations to Ryan and Luke for providing some magnificent insights into becoming a tennis player. By drawing on their own experiences as successful players and coaches, they provide us with the real truth on our game. A great read for parents and players.
— *Craig Tiley, Tennis Australia CEO and Australian Open tournament director*

Playing elite tennis can offer valuable life skills and provide a strong education and opportunities for networks, which can lay the foundations for a successful career. Navigating this path is difficult and *Winning On and Off the Court* is a valuable guide and resource for parents to help their children.
— *Mark Leschly, Universal Tennis Rating CEO*

Tennis is the toughest and most competitive individual sport in the world. The important balance between fun and hard work, sensible planning and obsession is a tricky one even for an experienced coach, let alone a parent new to the sport. This book is a must for coach, parent and player alike.
— *Pat Cash, former Wimbledon champion*

It's so important to develop the person holistically and instil character if you want a long career in tennis. Discipline and resilience may be the two defining characteristics that are most important provided you have the requisite skill set. Luke and Ryan present a balanced approach on the tennis journey. Success at any price is never worth it.
— *Wally Masur, former Davis Cup player and coach*

Love of tennis is a great and life-long gift for a parent to pass on to a child. It's not only a sport that can be thrilling to play and exciting to watch, but can provide enjoyable physical exercise into your seventies. Moreover, it can forge a very special bond: I remember my own father most fondly for his support of my early tennis ambitions and have tried to emulate them with my son. So, I can recognise the importance of this book, in which Ryan and Luke explain, clearly and wisely, how parental support can best be offered for mutual benefit, whether games are won or lost, or those dreams of centre court ever come true. Every tennis mum and dad should read it if they want their child to get the best from this terrific sport.
— *Geoffrey Robertson, Order of Australia, QC*

R3THINK PRESS

First published in Great Britain in 2019
by Rethink Press (www.rethinkpress.com)

© Copyright Ryan Henry and Luke Bourgeois

All rights reserved. No part of this publication may be reproduced, stored in or introduced into a retrieval system, or transmitted, in any form, or by any means (electronic, mechanical, photocopying, recording or otherwise) without the prior written permission of the publisher.

The right of Ryan Henry and Luke Bourgeois to be identified as the authors of this work has been asserted by them in accordance with the Copyright, Designs and Patents Act 1988.

This book is sold subject to the condition that it shall not, by way of trade or otherwise, be lent, resold, hired out, or otherwise circulated without the publisher's prior consent in any form of binding or cover other than that in which it is published and without a similar condition including this condition being imposed on the subsequent purchaser.

Wherever possible, permission has been obtained from the individuals concerned to reproduce their words and stories.

Disclaimer: The use of any information in this book, including any diet and nutrition plans, is solely at the reader's own risk. The authors and the publisher advise the reader to seek medical advice before undertaking any specific diet or nutrition plans.

Cover credit Copyright Shutterstock | Rashad Ashur

Contents

Foreword by John Fitzgerald	**1**
Introduction	**5**
Meet the authors	8
SECTION ONE An Overview Of The Tennis Journey	**11**
1 Why The Elite Tennis Journey?	**13**
The role of discipline in achieving success	15
Successful people often have competitive sporting backgrounds	17
Other life-enhancing opportunities	19
Summary	20
2 The Pivotal Role Of Parents	**21**
The number one influence	21
What parents can do	23
How parents can enhance the personal development of their children	28

The crucial moments on match day	30
The key behaviours	34
Some watch-outs	41
Summary	43

3 Achieving An Incredible Education Through Tennis — **45**

What is the attraction of a US college?	46
US intercollegiate sport	51
Tennis requirements for college scholarships	53
Mistakes to avoid	56
Choosing a high school that balances academic studies and tennis	59
Summary	62

4 The Power Of Setting Goals And Measuring Progress — **65**

Goal setting	66
Measuring the outcome	67
Developing goals and an action plan for your child	76
Summary	78

SECTION TWO Developing A Winning Tennis Game — **79**

5 Training — **81**

Hours on the court are the key to success	82
Evidence from tennis players	83
Training volume	86

Choosing a training environment   89
Summary   94

6 Match-Play Quantity   **97**

The benefits of match play   98
Target match-play quantities   102
Competitive opportunities   104
Preparing for match play   108
Factors that affect match conditions   110
Summary   118

SECTION THREE The Key Development Areas That Players Require   **119**

7 Developing A Winning Game   **121**

Understanding game styles   122
How to determine what game style is right for your child   125
Summary   132

8 Match-Play Tactics   **133**

Analysing opponents   133
Analysing the conditions   137
Developing and implementing match strategy   138
Summary   141

9 Good Technique And The Right Equipment   **143**

The role of the private coach   145
Achieving the optimal balance   152

Choosing the optimal equipment	153
Summary	162
10 Developing A High-Performance Athlete	**163**
Injury prevention	164
Joint and muscle mobility	167
Speed/agility	168
Strength	170
Endurance	172
Managing growth spurts	174
Summary	175
11 Fuelling A High-Performance Athlete	**177**
The food groups	180
Hydration	183
Main meals guide	184
Summary	185
12 Building Mental Toughness	**187**
A strong body leads to a strong mind	189
Concentration – the ability to sustain constant pressure on opponents	190
Dealing with adversity and negative emotions	193
Maintaining motivation	199
Summary	202

SECTION FOUR Where Can Tennis Lead?　　　　**203**

13 Becoming A Professional Tennis Player　　**205**

   How good does your child need to be
after high school to go pro?　　　　　　　　207

   The transition to pro tennis　　　　　　　　208

   The business of professional tennis　　　　210

   Doubles as a way to build a tennis career　213

   US college provides a platform for
going pro　　　　　　　　　　　　　　　　215

   Summary　　　　　　　　　　　　　　　　222

14 Life After Professional Tennis　　　　　　**223**

   Pursuing a career outside of tennis　　　　224

   Pursuing a career in tennis　　　　　　　　228

   Summary　　　　　　　　　　　　　　　　236

Acknowledgements　　　　　　　　　　　　**237**

References　　　　　　　　　　　　　　　　**241**

Further Reading　　　　　　　　　　　　　**251**

The Authors　　　　　　　　　　　　　　　**253**

Foreword
by John Fitzgerald

As a boy, I grew up on a wheat farm in the Eyre Peninsula, 650 km west of Adelaide in South Australia (SA). We had an old asphalt tennis court in my backyard where my two older brothers, who were among the best juniors in country SA, taught me how to play the game. My family was always proud of my tennis achievements and no matter how many tournaments I won, or what my world ranking was, the most important thing to them was that I worked hard, had integrity and stayed humble.

Being a former Davis Cup player and captain for Australia for several years has meant I've been fortunate enough to spend a lot of time with many of Australia's all-time greats of the game. Through all my years of involvement with the Australian squad,

I am proud to say that we had an incredible culture of hard work, honesty and mateship. Each individual thrived in this environment, being surrounded by great people.

Many of these players have gone on to have successful careers after retiring from the professional circuit, whether that be in business, politics or having critical roles in supporting the game of tennis.

The reality is that every tennis player has differing levels of potential, whether that's competing on the Association of Tennis Professionals/Women's Tennis Association (ATP/WTA) Tour, college or local club representation. The one thing that every player can strive towards is developing strong personal qualities and characteristics that can help them to become well rounded and successful in life in general.

From my experience from being in the game for over fifty years, my main observation is that the players who I most admire and respect as people have one common characteristic – they have parents who have a quality set of values who in turn instil those values in them.

Parents are at the coal face of their child's development and it's my view that they need to set their young player on the path of integrity. Parents also need the guidance of a coach who not only knows how to develop their youngster's tennis but can help mentor that same player to be of great ethical character.

FOREWORD BY JOHN FITZGERALD

I first came across Ryan and Luke when they were among the world's best juniors and then as professional players. They are two young Australians who surrounded themselves with good people who helped them to shape their character and ethics and they are living proof of the quality of people that tennis wants to have involved in our sport. What I really like about their Academy is that they have a strong philosophy and ambition to develop these desirable character traits in their students.

From their experiences as professional players and now coaches for many years, they are incredibly well positioned to provide players and parents with the crucial guidance they need to achieve the outcomes they want through the game.

I am a big believer that kids are a product of their family environment – parents who follow many of the suggestions in this book will give their child the best chance of becoming not only a better player, but also a great human as well.

John Fitzgerald, OAM Former Australian Davis Cup player and captain, world number one doubles player, winner of seven grand-slam doubles titles and recipient of the Medal of the Order of Australia

Introduction

> Tennis uses the language of life. 'Advantage', 'service', 'fault', 'break', and 'love'. The basic elements of tennis are those of everyday existence, because every match is a life in miniature.
> — Andre Agassi, eight-time grand-slam winner and philanthropist, *Open*, 2010

The journey to becoming an elite tennis player can be a hugely fulfilling one for parents and children, but there are many pitfalls and challenges that don't become apparent until you start it. This book is primarily about helping parents to foresee these challenges, manage them and maximise the joy in the game. It may be useful for players, at whatever stage of their career, and coaches, but it is mainly written with parents in mind.

Our belief from what we've seen throughout our careers is that tennis is a life-enhancing voyage and helps set students up for success.

> 'The keys to success in sport are very similar to the keys to success in business. You have to work very hard, you have to have a good process around how you prepare, how you focus… and train for the delivery of great outcomes.'[1]
> — Jayne Hrdlicka, President of Tennis Australia and CEO of a2 Milk

Parents are naturally assigned the responsibility of helping their child take advantage of the wonderful opportunity that tennis presents but navigating their child down this complex path can be challenging. There are literally thousands of decisions they need to make along the elite journey that have a huge effect on how far their child will go in tennis, and how successful they will become in life off the court. Parents' navigation of their child's tennis journey is often done without a map, background or experience in playing tennis at an elite level. This can lead to uncertainty over their child's future if they don't find the right balance between tennis and education. Below average tennis outcomes are commonplace, and some families experience burnout through training and competition schedules that significantly impact their lifestyle.

---

1   Darren Gray, 'When Jayne met Roger: How tennis legend inspired new a2 Milk boss', *The Sydney Morning Herald* (2018) www.smh.com.au/business/companies/when-jayne-met-roger-how-tennis-legend-inspired-new-a2-milk-boss-20180731-p4zupe.html

INTRODUCTION

It doesn't have to be that way.

This book is the map that guides parents to navigate the tennis pathway so that their child is provided with every opportunity to be successful both on and, importantly, off the court. It will show parents how to get the right balance of tennis and education, and how to make this pathway one of the most rewarding experiences for both themselves and their child. It doesn't provide all the answers, but hopefully it will assist families in making the right decisions for their child. We are passionate about tennis juniors having the opportunity to access a US college education, and this book will help parents to understand what they require to make this happen.

The first section of this book is about making parents aware of the opportunities available for their child within tennis, their own critical role, and how to balance tennis and education successfully so that their child is provided with every opportunity to be successful on and off the court.

The second section shares the importance of the volume of hours on the training court and how critical match play is for the child to achieve their goals.

The third section goes through all the essential areas players need to work on as it discusses the importance of nutrition and physical, psychological, technical and tactical development.

The final section contains details on how to navigate the pro circuit, as well as career options within and outside the game.

Meet the authors

Ryan Henry and Luke Bourgeois understand the elite-player journey from first-hand experience, being ex-pros who have worked with hundreds of tennis players, many of whom have played for US colleges or gone on to play professional tennis.

Tennis has created some life-enhancing opportunities for Ryan and Luke – such as travelling the world and competing in grand slams – and given them many lifelong friends and incredible personal development. It has also enabled them to build, run and grow a thriving tennis academy in Sydney.

In the book, they share some of the things that have worked well for both of them, some regrets, and a lot of experience they have picked up from mentors and coaches such as Tony Roche, Kim Warwick, Roger Federer, John Newcombe, Wally Masur, Chris Kachel, Graeme Brimblecombe, Mark McGrath, Richard Fromberg, John McCurdy and Jaime McDonagh.

Their belief is that tennis can be a powerful, life-enhancing voyage that helps an individual become the best person they can be. They want to impart their

INTRODUCTION

love and 'way' for the game of tennis, inspiring, educating and coaching players to give them the best possible tennis development, education and life-skills to help them succeed in whatever they decide to do in life.

Within this book, you will find a number of references to PDF templates. You can find these at http://voyagertennis.com/blog

SECTION ONE
AN OVERVIEW OF THE TENNIS JOURNEY

Tennis teaches you all the important things, all the things you need to know. ... It teaches you to stand on your own, to be patient, to know that there are going to be losses, and to learn from those losses.
— Peter Burwash, former professional tennis player, *Tennis Industry Magazine*, 2010

1
Why The Elite Tennis Journey?

> If you watch someone on the court for five minutes, you'll get to know all about them. You'll get to see what their value structure is, you'll get to see their character.
> — Peter Burwash, *Tennis Industry Magazine*, 2010

> Love of tennis is a great and lifelong gift for a parent to pass on to a child. It's not only a sport that can be thrilling to play and exciting to watch, but can provide enjoyable physical exercise into your seventies. Moreover, it can forge a very special bond: I remember my own father most fondly for his support of my early tennis ambitions and have tried to emulate them with my son.
> — Geoffrey Robertson, Queen's Counsel

Pursuing tennis at an elite level can be one of the most exciting and rewarding journeys a person can go on. The buzz of competing against the best can be hugely enjoyable for both players and their parents, but even more important are the human qualities that tennis provides to players from their experiences on the court and the dedication and self-discipline they require off the court. The thrill of competing often brings every human emotion possible to the surface. Players who strive to reach world class levels of the game also develop an incredibly strong work ethic and the personal qualities they need to be successful in any area of life.

Tennis breeds a sense of responsibility and self-ownership. Players must learn to be accountable for the results they get and go to work to adjust their approach as and when required. In many team sports, it is possible for players to hide behind teammates, but in tennis this is simply not the case. Even doubles, where players compete as a team, requires a high level of personal commitment to achieve positive outcomes.

Through their effort to realise their potential and become the best they can be, elite tennis players will often develop many of the following personal qualities:

- Discipline, a strong work ethic, a growth mindset, perseverance, respect
- Integrity, ability to handle stress and adversity, self-control, sportsmanship, ability to focus for extended periods of time
- Problem-solving skills, goal setting and achieving mindset, time-management skills, determination, courage

These lists show a number of fine human qualities, but probably the most important of all of these is discipline as it is the foundation that successful people build on across all industries. Discipline can set players up not only for an elite tennis career, but also for life after tennis.

The role of discipline in achieving success

> All great success in life is preceded by long, sustained periods of focused effort on a single goal... with the determination to stay with it until it is complete.
> — Brian Tracy, motivational speaker, success coach and best-selling author

Fortunately, the quality of self-discipline is something you can develop by continuous practice in an environment that encourages it. Elite tennis training environments develop self-discipline rapidly.

CASE STUDY – RYAN'S CHARACTER-BUILDING EXPERIENCE IN THE AUSTRALIAN INSTITUTE OF SPORT

At the age of fifteen I was offered a scholarship with the Australian Institute of Sport (AIS). The AIS was the most elite tennis programme in Australia where all of the highest ranked players were trained by the best coaches at the top facilities in the country. During that period, the programme had invited sixteen players across two age groups, scheduling a number of player cuts so that there would only be six players remaining in the programme by the beginning of the following year.

I felt my chances of making the top six weren't great. I'd grown up in a laid-back coastal town, Pacific Palms in NSW, with a population fewer than 3,000 people, and had little exposure to demanding environments like the AIS. My coaches when I was a young junior told me that I didn't train hard or consistently enough, or that I was lazy and my natural talent would only take me so far.

The first twelve months in the AIS programme were the hardest and most brutal I'd had up to that point. Training was incredibly long and tough and pushed me to my absolute limits on many occasions. Coaches expected 110% effort and simply didn't tolerate excuses. Often when I thought the day was over, they scheduled another training session, or if the group stayed up too late, we'd get a knock on the door at five the next morning with training commencing immediately to teach us a lesson. Anybody who was late for a session was punished heavily with extra physical training. This happened to me multiple times in the beginning until I understood the importance of being on time. The group was also regularly reminded that several players were not going to make the cut, which was another catalyst for me to push the boundaries of my comfort zone and work ethic every day.

Twelve months later, after a lot of hard work and changing of bad habits, I managed to make the cut as one of the top six players chosen to stay on in the AIS. After three years in that high-pressure environment, I'd achieved a world number one ranking in 18/U doubles and number sixteen in the world in 18/U singles. I was competing in the Men's Australian Open main draw singles and doubles in front of thousands of people and the television cameras.

The environment the coaches in the AIS created caused me to push myself harder than I ever thought I would every day and eventually transformed me from being lazy into a professional with a world class work ethic and discipline. These personal qualities allowed me to rapidly develop my game and compete against the best players in the world, which is why I feel so strongly about the value of an elite tennis environment to develop discipline and character in an individual.

Successful people often have competitive sporting backgrounds

According to *Business Insider,* many of America's most successful CEOs started out in sports before entering and dominating the world of business, and according to theceomagazine.com, up to 95% of Fortune 500 CEOs played competitive sports in their childhood. [2]/[3]

The link between competitive sport and business is equally strong for men and women. A 2015 study of 400 female C-suite executives conducted by espnW and EY found an overwhelming correlation between athletic and business success: 94% of women in the C-suite played sports. Of the 94%, more than half (52%) played at a university level, compared to 39% of women at lower management levels. The same study also found that 80% of female Fortune 500 executives played competitive sports. These studies show that competitive tennis was among the top three most common sports that successful business executives played in their childhood.

People who have been exposed to high-level sport often have the ability to handle adversity and stress, which is essential in the business world, more effectively than those who have not.

Venus Williams cites the experiences she had in tennis as being key for her as she builds her business career. She is the founder and CEO of the clothing

---

2 Kathleen Elkins, 'These 9 successful CEOs all played sports in college' (2015) www.businessinsider.com.au/successful-ceos-who-played-sports-in-college-2015-2?r=US&IR=T#ge-ceo-jeffrey-immelt-played-football-for-dartmouth-1
3 CEO Magazine, 'A look at the link between playing sports and success in business' (2018) www.theceomagazine.com/business/management-leadership/look-link-playing-sports-success-business

line, EleVen, and interior design company, V Starr Interiors.

> 'I think as an athlete you're always overcoming all kinds of challenges... So definitely applying those lessons of perseverance and learning from mistakes and setting goals has definitely helped me in business.'[4]
> — Venus Williams, talking to *Forbes* magazine

Other life-enhancing opportunities

Besides character development, tennis can provide many other benefits. Some of the most common reasons why parents get their children involved in elite tennis are:

- Tennis is a fun game that they will often be able to play into old age
- It offers a heathy environment away from the negative influences that can occur during teenage years
- It furthers their education via opportunities such as US college tennis scholarships
- It develops a huge circle of like-minded friends

---

4   Mia Saini, 'Venus Williams: A Force Off The Court' (2010) www.forbes.com/sites/face-to-face/2010/08/02/venus-williams-a-force-off-the-court/#2cd047b4c55a

- It enables children to travel the world and experience many different cultures and people
- It provides the opportunity to become a professional tennis player

Summary

Tennis is a game that both builds and reveals a person's character. The qualities of independence, resilience and self-discipline that tennis players develop will stand them in good stead throughout their careers and lives.

2
The Pivotal Role Of Parents

> As important as the coach's role is, the tennis parent's role is tenfold more important.
> — Nick Bollettieri, tennis coach of Andre Agassi, Monica Seles, Boris Becker, *Australian Tennis Magazine*, 2011

> My biggest influence was my mother; she is my life mentor.
> — Martina Hingis, former world number one and winner of twenty-five grand-slam titles, Tennis.com, 2015

The number one influence

The role that parents play in ensuring that their child's tennis journey is fulfilling for their personal development and tennis career cannot be underestimated. It will be challenging, time consuming, pressured, at times stressful, but managed the right way, it can also be enormously rewarding.

Through our years' experience as players and coaches, we have found that parents have far and away the most influence on how much success and enjoyment their children gain from tennis, much more than an individual coach or an academy. This is supported by research that shows that a parent's interaction with their child is far more influential than non-parent interactions.[5]

This book aims to help parents navigate the tennis-parenting journey as effectively as possible. To have the greatest positive impact, parents have two broad roles:

- What they do – the tasks parents do with and for their child

- How they interact with their child – how they go about guiding and supporting their child is just as important as what they do

This chapter gives an introduction to the whats and the hows, exploring the things that parents need to be aware of in a junior tennis player's journey, then we will go into more detail in subsequent chapters. We also recommended that parents read *The Tennis Parent's*

---

5   J. Cassidy and P. R. Shaver, *Handbook of Attachment: Theory, Research, and Clinical Applications* (Guildford Press, 2018)

Bible by Frank Giampaolo, which is a comprehensive guide focusing on building champion tennis players.

Of course, there may be parents who drive their child so hard that while the child may achieve success on the tennis court, it comes at the price of a fractured relationship. The approach we recommend maintains a harmonious relationship and alignment between parents and child.

What parents can do

Parents are by default the ultimate decision makers responsible for overseeing many crucial factors that can make or break a player's tennis career. This can be incredibly challenging, particularly for parents without elite tennis or coaching backgrounds. Making mistakes in just one area can be detrimental for your child's progress, so this book aims to provide you with a deep level of understanding so that you can effectively support your child, ask the right questions and make informed decisions.

Some of the key areas that parents need to provide strong guidance on are:

Balancing tennis and education

When a player reaches high school, their tennis and academic requirements increase at the same time, which can create significant pressure on the family's time and resources. Parents need to work out how to balance both, so their child can achieve their tennis and academic goals.

Most elite players are now pursuing US college tennis scholarships, which typically require individuals to be A+ tennis players and B/C grade students to be eligible. Getting the balance right here can provide students with an incredible education and set them up for life.

Setting goals and measuring progress

Top-level athletes, successful businesspeople and high achievers in all fields set goals. When an individual sets challenging but realistic goals, it can increase motivation, encourage them to work harder and help them organise their time and resources to maximise their potential. Parents need to encourage their child to become a goal setter and regularly measure progress to ensure they are on the road to achievement.

Creating an on-court training plan

Once the child has a clear vision for their long-term goals, their parents need to construct a training plan that aligns with the achievement of those goals. This includes squad training, practice and private lessons.

Studies carried out at our own Academy with over 100 elite tennis players show that a structured training plan produces predictable long-term results. A low training volume coincides with a lower playing standard, while a high training volume reflects a high playing standard. Parents need to construct a weekly plan that provides their child with an appropriate number of hours on court.

Tournament/match-play scheduling

A player's match-play history is perhaps the strongest determinant of their success in tennis. Our research shows that players who have competed in many matches vastly outperform those who haven't. Parents need to create a tournament and match-play plan that aligns with their child's long-term goals.

Tactics

Some of the most critical tactical areas that a player needs to develop are ensuring they are playing the right game style for their physical characteristics, effectively analysing opponents, and the ability to create and implement match strategies. The private coach/mentor that the parents select will usually play a big role in the tactical development of their child.

Technical foundations

It's really important for players to establish good technical foundations at a young age. This will enable them to continually reproduce a shot without error and execute a wide variety of tactics against an opponent. Players with technical deficiencies tend to have strokes that break down under pressure and weaknesses that their opponents will be able to exploit. Parents need to find a suitably qualified coach who can help with this area while being a great mentor throughout the child's elite-player journey.

Physical development

Most elite tennis players will need their body to perform on the court for a couple of decades. With tennis being a repetitive sport, parents need to be aware of the importance of athletes looking after their bodies. Maintaining an injury-free status must be the top priority; enhancing physical qualities such as speed, endurance and power are important, but they come second. Parents need to ensure their child has had a physical screening and has a regular pre-habilitation and physical development programme in place.

Nutrition

A healthy nutrition plan provides the fuel an athlete needs to perform at a high level day in, day out. Parents play an essential role in their child's nutrition as they are often the ones shopping, cooking the meals and packing the lunches. They need to provide their child with the right balance of the main food groups (carbohydrates, protein and fats) and good hydration, as well as discouraging them from food and drinks that will have a negative impact on performance.

Psychology

Tennis is one of the most challenging sports when it comes to psychology. Players need to develop key mental skills such as the ability to concentrate, deal with negative emotions and maintain long-term motivation. Parents need to be aware that these skills are rarely innate and must be developed over time, potentially with the help of an expert in this area.

Going to college or becoming professional

Players who are pursuing the professional pathway will need to decide whether to go pro immediately after high school or pursue options such as the US college tennis pathway first. The reality is that 99% of elite players will have a much better chance of playing professionally if they go to college first as these four extra years of tennis development are crucial. Parents who are approaching this decision need to pay particularly close attention to Chapter 13.

The remainder of the book goes into more depth about each of these areas with dedicated chapters. There are so many things to consider that it may seem overwhelming, but if you understand each of these areas, do some planning and access the right level of support, it is manageable.

How parents can enhance the personal development of their children

> As a tennis player, you have to get used to losing every week... But you have to take the positive out of a defeat and go back to work.
> — Stanislas Wawrinka, winner of three grand-slam titles, *Forbes*, 2014

Tennis must be one of the most challenging sports for competitors to deal with. Think about a weekend tournament with a draw of sixty-four players. At the end of the tournament, there is only one winner and sixty-three losers – a staggering 98% of players will lose. If you compare that to a weekend game of competitive soccer, only eleven players out of the twenty-two can lose, and all twenty-two may come away with a draw. Tennis is a gladiatorial sport that can be lonely, but it is also one where players can learn to deal with adversity and build resilience.

Why is it so hard to be a good tennis parent?

Your communication as a parent is the most powerful determinant of your child's mental and character development. Parents have a crucial role in helping to build their child's resilience on and off the tennis court and it's easy to underestimate how hard it is to be a 'good' tennis parent. You need to be able to control your own emotions and be a supportive role model for your child.

Many parents instinctively know the right actions and behaviours to communicate to their child in a tennis setting, yet most have difficulty with implementation. Watching your child play tennis can be like watching your own DNA run around a court and compete, so it's difficult to separate yourself from your emotions in the heat of a match to provide support. Parents will often describe feeling the same types and intensity of emotion as their child, the only difference being that the child can take action while the parent has to sit outside the court, helpless to influence the outcome of the match.

A parent watching their child play can often experience heightened emotions such as anger and frustration when they need to be displaying neutral or supportive body language if their child looks their way after losing a point. Likewise, after a lost match, a parent may be experiencing intense negative emotions, but at the same time they need to be supportive and provide unconditional love. The post-match moment is often a difficult one for both player and parent.

Knowledge combined with practice will hopefully lead you to becoming a tennis parent who has a strong and positive impact on your child.

The crucial moments on match day

Frank Giampaolo in his book *The Tennis Parent's Bible* puts it succinctly: on match days, the primary role of parents is to de-stress their child.[6]

Match days can be very stressful and stressed athletes can be fearful, which increases muscle contractions, impairing movement, judgement and problem-solving skills. Tennis players perform best in calm, relaxed mental states.

Pre-match preparation

Aside from creating an environment that is as stress-free as possible, parents can also guide their child through developing a match plan (which we expand upon in Chapter 8), their nutrition and hydration requirements, and establishing warm-up routines. It's important to note the parents' role here is to guide

---

[6] F. Giampaolo, *The Tennis Parent's Bible: Second Edition* (CreateSpace Independent Publishing Platform, 2016)

their child to create a plan, not do all the planning for them.

During the match

It's incredibly difficult not to get caught up in the emotions of a match, so one way to distance yourself is to focus on analysing the match. Evaluate dispassionately how your child is playing relative to their match plan alongside their technical, tactical, physical and mental performance. There are a number of apps available which you can use to statistically analyse your child's performance.

Post-match communication

There are certain times when your child's mind is open to being influenced, and as a parent you need to be aware of this. There are two important times to consider when your child's character development is most easily influenced.

The first is when your child is experiencing high levels of emotion. Research has shown that when an experience is unemotional, our brain doesn't remember it with much strength, but when an experience arouses high levels of emotion, our brain recognises it as important and becomes more plastic and easily rewired.[7] This is the foundation for how we remember things.

The second critical time is after exercise. Through evolution, we have been primed to recognise experiences following exercise as important to remember, and the brain is then much more open to being rewired and influenced.

The messages you communicate (either verbally or non-verbally) when your child is experiencing high levels of emotion, or post exercise, will have a much bigger influence on them than at any other time. A perfect example of both situations would be when your child comes off the court after a long tennis match, particularly when they've lost.

There are two crucial messages that you can communicate during this period that will be of great benefit to your child's character and self-esteem:

- That your love for them is unconditional and not dependent on whether they won or lost the match
- That you believe their effort rather than performance will pay off in the long term

---

7   James L. McGaugh, 'The Amygdala Modulates the Consolidation of Memories of Emotionally Arousing Experiences', *Annual Review of Neuroscience* (2004) www.annualreviews.org/doi/abs/10.1146/annurev.neuro.27.070203.144157

When you're communicating these messages, consider that your child will also be picking up on all of your non-verbal communications such as eye contact, facial expressions, tone of voice, body position, gesturing, and the timing and intensity of your responses. That is why it's important that your verbal and non-verbal communications are aligned.

There are some things that you can do to help manage this:

- Prior to the end of the match, go through a mental checklist of how you want to behave. Have a routine that is the same, no matter a loss or a win, whether that is a high five, a hug, or whatever else works for you and your child.

- Use questions to find out what your child learned from the match after they have had time to settle down from the post-match euphoria or despondency. Ask them:

    - What did you learn about your game?

    - What did you learn about your opponent?

    - How well did you execute your game plan?

    - How was your body language?

    - How was your attitude on court?

    - Out of ten, how much effort did you put in?

- If you can write down the learnings, that's great, but always finish by emphasising the positives with words of encouragement.

As tennis parents, you will no doubt have seen some behaviour that is different from this. We have seen a lot of extreme behaviour, such as a parent coming on court and smashing their child's racquets, shouting at their child, or driving off in disgust and leaving their child to make their own way home. We don't condone this, of course, but it shows how invested parents can become and how difficult it is in the heat of the moment to behave supportively. Hopefully, our tips will help.

Beyond managing the post-match cauldron of emotions, you will encounter a number of other times where how you interact with your child will be as important as what you do. We will now cover some of the key behaviours that can help develop your child into a strong, resilient and independent person.

The key behaviours

Being supportive

Tennis is one of the most challenging sports when it comes to dealing with adversity and the range of intense emotions that come with it. Parents need to do their best to understand what their child is going through and communicate with empathy before giving advice. This can increase a child's self-esteem and make them feel that they are important and understood.

To provide the appropriate levels of emotional support, the key is balance. It is equally detrimental to be either under supportive or over involved.

Reflect on what your motivations are regarding your child's tennis. Parents who are in it to provide personal development opportunities for their child are more likely to promote enjoyment and increase long-term motivation, whereas parents whose primary motivation is for their child to become a professional tennis player often create a stressful environment that can lead to their child enjoying the game less. Ultimately, this can mean the child leaves the sport altogether.

There are many different approaches to being a 'good' tennis parent – it is definitely not one size fits all. The following example is not typical, but it worked for Luke's father.

CASE STUDY – LUKE'S FATHER'S APPROACH

I didn't realise it at the time, but I was really fortunate to be the youngest of ten children as it meant my parents had pretty much seen it all before and were incredibly relaxed about everything by the time I came along. An example that jumps to mind is when I was competing in one of my first professional tournaments in Corfu, Greece. I had made the quarter-finals of the singles and it was one of the most important matches of my career to that point.

My father happened to be travelling in Europe at that time and thought it would be a good idea to drop in and watch me play. Due to having nine other children, he'd rarely had the chance to watch me compete before and it was nice to have him finally attend a match.

The match was incredibly hard-fought and it all came down to the third set tiebreaker. It was 6–6 and whoever won this point was going to have a match point. I was really nervous and decided to look to my dad for support. When I glanced at him, I couldn't believe what I saw.

He was sleeping!

I was stunned, and a little amused that my dad could fall asleep in one of the most important moments of my career. I lost the next two points and the match. Naturally disappointed with the loss, I decided not to disturb my dad's sleep and went to lunch instead. When I came back to see him, he was still happily sleeping by the court.

This is an insight into how little pressure and stress my parents put on me to perform. They just let me do my thing, which was great and gave me the space to decide what I wanted and forge my own path.

There are unfortunately many high-profile examples in Australia and around the world of tennis parents behaving poorly, being overbearing and not role modelling the appropriate behaviour. Consequently, their child suffers.

Be a role model

There is a well-known saying that actions speak louder than words, and this is definitely the case when it comes to parenting. Your child will listen to some of what you say while copying most of your actions and behaviours, and as a result will become similar to you in many ways when they're a parent. To expect otherwise would be unrealistic. It is important that parents are great role models when it comes to taking responsibility for outcomes, working hard, providing calm responses to emotional situations while regulating determination and enjoyment of competition.

Encourage resilience

To be successful in anything in life, you need to be able to develop mental toughness and handle adversity. An important aspect here is to expose your child to challenging environments. This allows them to experience adversity and promotes opportunities for them to adapt, grow and become resilient.

A mistake that some parents make is spoiling their child, being over protective and not providing enough opportunities for their child to work hard and overcome difficulties. This is likely to lead to the child becoming helpless when they're facing adversity during a match. Parents who operate on the tougher side of the spectrum allow their child to develop the ability to overcome tough situations on the court.

Develop your child's self-esteem and self-belief

It's vitally important that parents communicate unconditional love and acceptance of their child, regardless of match outcomes or performance. This helps build the child's self-esteem and results in them having a balanced approach to competition. Parents who communicate love conditionally on results will lower the self-esteem of their child and increase the child's anxiety regarding results.

You need to be encouraging and positive with a focus on competence along with ability to achieve future goals. Consistent positive communication will provide opportunities to increase your child's self-belief, which encourages them to challenge themselves and go after the joy that comes with achieving. Parents who are negative and critical with regard to their child's performances promote self-doubt and self-criticism. Expectations are another important element in building self-confidence in your child. Parents who communicate high expectations encourage their child to overcome challenges and develop self-belief.

It is important to strike a balance between the two extremes of communicating low expectations, which promote low self-belief and low drive to achieve, and unrealistically high expectations, which increase anxiety and continual frustration and disappointment with performance.

Encourage decision making and independence

It's important for your child to feel a level of autonomy and buy in when it comes to making decisions. Let them decide to play the game and excel in it because they love it. As a parent, you can encourage this, particularly if you have a love for the game yourself. Ultimately you want to make your child feel like they are in complete control of their destiny and are incredibly supported along the way.

Problem solving needs to be a regular part of your child's development, so it's important not to do the thinking for them. Encourage your child to solve problems and make decisions. Parents who do everything for their child or give them all the answers can promote helplessness.

Encourage autonomy at developmentally appropriate ages in conjunction with the balance of setting clear limits, boundaries and consequences for poor behaviour. When the child doesn't meet certain standards, apply appropriate consequences consistently. This teaches a child that their actions are important and will guide appropriate behaviours and values.

CASE STUDY – PARENTS OF ELITE PLAYER MICHAELA (MICKI) HAET

Mark and Malaine Haet are great examples of tennis parents who have done an amazing job with their daughter Michaela (Micki). As a result, she has become a world class player and person at the same time.

Micki's father Mark played competitive tennis as a junior and attended and graduated from Duke University in the United States, which he thoroughly enjoyed. This gave Mark and Malaine the idea to give their daughter Micki all the opportunities she needed to reach a level where she could play college tennis in the United States – if that was what Micki wanted to do. Each year when she was a junior, Mark and Malaine would help her put together a good-quality weekly programme balancing school work with a high volume of practice hours on court, and they'd travel with her to tournaments on weekends and school holidays.

Micki started to get noticed when she achieved the number one ranking in Australia for the 14/U age group. She was then invited into the Tennis Australia's National Academy programme, which provided even more quality opportunities for her to practise along with physical, psychological and tournament support services.

Upon graduating from high school, she won two WTA futures events and achieved a WTA world ranking of 521 before going to college. In her first year in college, Micki was the number one ranked freshman recruit of all female players in the United States and was offered several scholarship opportunities to attend some amazing colleges. In the end, she decided to accept an offer to play for and attend Rice University in Texas, which is considered one of the best colleges in the United States.

At the time of writing, Micki is in her second year of college and is having the time of her life. Perhaps the most rewarding part of watching Micki grow over the years has been seeing the person that she's become. She's confident, has an excellent work ethic, is personable and positive, and has every chance of being successful in whatever she chooses to do in life. This has everything to do with Mark and Malaine's supportive and positive parenting style.

Malaine says, 'Mark and I have had some of our most memorable and exciting life moments watching Micki grow and develop through her tennis and test herself in competition. We've always let her be the decision maker and sought guidance from her coaches, just being there to support her in any way that we can. What's really rewarding for us is seeing how much she's grown as a person since going to college and how close we all are as a family.'

Some watch-outs

I'm sure you can think of a professional player with low values who is unpopular and a poor role model for the next generation of kids looking up to them. Most of the time, their behaviours can be traced back to the parents, who are responsible for tennis parenting in a certain way throughout the player's childhood.

If you'd like your child to grow up as a happy, strong and confident individual who loves their elite tennis journey, avoid the following behaviours:

- Making no effort to understand what your child is going through emotionally and physically, and consequently communicating with a lack of empathy
- Spoiling or overprotecting your child and not providing enough challenging opportunities for them to face and overcome adversity
- Communicating love only when your child is doing well or winning
- Communicating negatively and pessimistically to your child with regard to their skills and abilities
- Communicating low expectations to your child
- Communicating unrealistically high expectations to your child
- Discouraging independence and making all the decisions for your child
- Being a poor role model and expecting your child to be different (the 'do as I say and not as I do' approach doesn't work well)

You've probably been doing everything you possibly can to give your child the best chance of becoming successful. Many parents dedicate huge amounts of time, energy and resources to getting their child to training and tournaments, which often means making considerable lifestyle sacrifices. Now is the time to invest in understanding and implementing best-practice tennis parenting to help shape your child into a person you can be proud of.

Summary

Being a tennis parent is incredibly challenging and testing at times, and it can be difficult to know whether you are doing the right thing. What a parent does to foster their child's journey and how they do it will have an enormous impact on the success of the child's tennis career and their wellbeing.

Actions to consider:

- Take time to look at the objectives you and your child have for tennis.

- Read widely and talk to other parents and coaches who have experience in guiding players successfully down the elite tennis path.

- Reflect on what sort of tennis parent you want to be.

- Put in place post-match routines with your child that help you both manage intense emotions.

3
Achieving An Incredible Education Through Tennis

> We really both feel that our two years at Stanford were the best two years of our lives.
> — Bob Bryan, who – with brother Mike – made up the most successful male doubles team in tennis history, *The Stanford Daily*, 2016

It almost goes without saying that ensuring their child gets a good education is one of the primary aims of most parents. Education is a key factor that enables a person to enter and succeed in a career, so pursuing tennis at the expense of an education is rarely a worthwhile exercise.

This chapter outlines the opportunity that tennis gives to gain a higher education at a US college funded by an athletic scholarship, providing a great platform for going professional if that is your child's ambition.

What is the attraction of a US college?

US college sport is difficult to comprehend fully unless you have attended a college sporting event. Facilities and crowd attendances can be similar to professional sporting events, with college tennis matches sometimes having over 1,000 spectators, depending on which college it is. Playing in this environment is a phenomenal experience for your child.

The amount of resources that American universities offer is enormous, ranging from state-of-the-art tennis facilities to coaches, fitness trainers, athletics trainers, nutritionists, sports psychologists, academic tutors, academic advisors and more. All of these resources are put in place for the student athlete to maximise their chances at being successful academically as well as on the court. Many top players competed in college sports, including John Isner, John McEnroe, Kevin Anderson, James Blake, Mike and Bob Bryan, and more recently Danielle Collins who made the semi-finals of the women's singles in the 2019 Australian Open.

A university education is a great leg up in life. Research shows that a person with a university qualification will earn an average of AU$31,200 more per year over the course of their career than a person who finishes their education after high school. This equates to more than AU$1 million in extra income over a person's working life.[8] When we look at these statistics, it becomes an easy choice for parents to encourage their child to pursue this type of education.

For those looking to play on the professional circuit, there is even more evidence to encourage them to do it via a US college education. Twenty or thirty years ago it was much easier to move from high school to playing on the professional tour. There were a lot fewer players competing for places on the ATP/WTA tour, so it was quite common for top juniors to finish high school, do well in a couple of satellites and challenger events, and be in the top 100 in the world twelve to eighteen months later.

This rarely happens now due to the rapid rise in the number of players pursuing professional tennis and the increasing physicality of the modern game. For those who do make the top 100, it now takes an average of four years from the time they begin competing professionally, with the average age of players in the top 100 being twenty-eight for men and twenty-six for women.

An eighteen-year-old who has just completed high school will find it almost impossible to compete successfully at the higher levels on the professional tour due to a number of factors, including a lack of court

---

8   Conal Hanna, 'A university degree is worth $1,180,112 over the course of a lifetime' (2017) www.smh.com.au/money/a-university-degree-is-worth-1180112-over-the-course-of-a-lifetime-20171026-gz8mgd.html

time and not being physically and mentally mature enough to compete against professionals who are often ten years older and far more experienced. In today's game, many of the world's best eighteen to twenty-two-year-old players are going pro via the US college pathway. That way, they can get a degree while seeing if they have what it takes to get on the ATP/WTA tour at the age of twenty-two, by which time they are more physically and mentally mature and have had an extra four years to develop their tennis. After college, if a player attempts to go pro and realises they don't have the game to crack the top 100, then they have a degree behind them, along with some unforgettable life experiences and a strong character, all of which provide a fantastic foundation for a successful career either inside or outside of tennis.

Some of the main benefits of US colleges compared to other university systems are:

- Through scholarships, tennis players can earn a degree at a much cheaper cost than universities in other countries.

- Students don't have to decide what they want to study by the end of Year 12. Instead, they can decide in their second year at college.

- The opportunity to study exclusive degrees like law or medicine is available to most students. In many countries, these degrees are available only for the top 1% or 2% of students. In the United

States, once you are accepted into a college, you are free to choose what course you'd like to study.

CASE STUDY - JEREMY BOURGEOIS

A good example of a player who pursued the US college pathway is Jeremy Bourgeois (Luke's nephew). Jeremy was a solid nationally ranked junior tennis player in Sydney, which really helped him to get into the Brigham Young University (BYU) in Utah. This university has one of the top ten finance programmes in the United States.

Jeremy had the best time of his life in college, but realised at the end of it that his tennis wasn't good enough to enable him to compete successfully at the highest level on the pro circuit. He graduated from BYU with a major in economics and a minor in business management and decided that it was time to move back to Sydney and start developing his career.

He applied for a job at one of Australia's largest banks, Macquarie Bank. The fact he'd been a student athlete at a US college made his CV stand out from the rest of the 100+ applicants and he got the call for an interview soon after.

The first thing his prospective employer wanted to know was who Jeremy was, gaining some insight into his life experiences and education to date. Jeremy expanded on his background as an elite tennis player and his experience as a student athlete living in the United States for four years, which involved managing a full athletic programme (twenty hours a week with training and gym) and a lot of travel at weekends to compete against other university teams, all while studying. The prospective employer realised that Jeremy must have good discipline and time-management skills and a strong achievement-driven character. After his first interview, he was offered the job, and now has an incredible opportunity to move his way up at one of Australia's biggest and most successful financial institutions.

Jeremy tells us in his own words why his US college experience was so powerful:

'Most of the other applicants that I was up against graduated from Australian universities, and to my employer, on paper they all look similar. My student athlete experience in the United States was different to anybody else's, which stood out and contributed enormously to me landing the job with Macquarie.

'My new role with its demanding sales targets is similar to competing in tennis. I've brought my competitive nature into what I am doing now, which has served me really well so far.'

If they're working towards their child getting a US college education, parents need to consider several things during their child's schooling. The overarching requirement is that the vast majority of Division 1 colleges are looking for A+ tennis players who are B/C students, so those who can get this balance right will generally have the most college opportunities and biggest scholarship offers.

If your child is an elite-level tennis player by the time they graduate from high school, they can achieve a US college tennis scholarship at some of the best universities in the world. These scholarships can be worth up to US$400,000 over a four-year period. A typical scholarship will cover tutoring and academic support, racquets, clothes sponsorship, travel around the United States, food and accommodation off campus, massage and physiotherapy, along with a percentage of tuition, books, on-campus housing and food.

Parents living in countries outside the United States might be thinking that it's almost too good to be true and wondering why colleges would invest so much in the tennis athletes. To help you understand this better, we'll now paint a picture of how big college sport is in the United States.

US intercollegiate sport

College sport in the United States is a big business that has been around since the 1840s and has a large economic impact on the schools themselves and their surrounding communities. There are a number of US colleges that have football stadiums with capacities of over 100,000 people which are full during both home and away games, producing substantial revenue from ticket and merchandise sales and broadcast contracts. As an example, the University of Texas's football programme, the most valuable in-college sports, makes an average of US$93 million per year.[9] The National Collegiate Athletic Association (NCAA) earned US$989 million in revenue in 2014 from television, advertising and licensing revenue, and the schools benefit from ticket and merchandising sales and donations.[10] As a result, American colleges invest a huge amount of resources in their sporting facilities, coaches and athletes.

To give you an idea of how much some colleges are willing to invest, as of 2018, the highest paid National Football League college football coach was Nick Saban – $11,132,000 from the University of Alabama – and the highest paid basketball coach was John Calipari – $7,450,00 from the University of Kentucky.[11]

As you can see, intercollegiate sport is a huge business in the United States, and elite tennis players from countries all around the world can benefit from this. In the United States, there are over 24 million students enrolled in around 4,500 colleges, with about 800,000 of these being international students. In 2019, around 950 of these colleges had tennis scholarships available

---

9 Chris Smith, 'College Football's Most Valuable Teams', *Forbes* (2018) www.forbes.com/sites/chrissmith/2018/09/11/college-footballs-most-valuable-teams/#7975f5016c64
10 Kevin McGuire, 'NCAA revenue jumps closer to $1 billion' (2015) http://collegefootballtalk.nbcsports.com/2015/03/11/ncaa-revenue-jumps-closer-to-1-billion
11 Bobby Rich, 'The 25 Highest-Paid College Coaches of 2019', *The Quad* (2019) https://thebestschools.org/magazine/highest-paid-college-coaches

for men and about 1,100 had tennis scholarships available for women.[12]

As we're sure you can imagine, the choice of colleges can be daunting, and the application process is extensive. Fortunately, there are specialists who can guide you through this process and take on some of the time-consuming elements, ensuring you don't make any mistakes that could make your child ineligible.

Tennis requirements for college scholarships

The importance of UTR

College coaches now use the universal tennis rating (UTR) as their main tool for recruiting players into their teams (see www.myutr.com). Any player who is serious about going to college needs to know what their UTR is and what UTR they need to achieve in order to go to their desired college. For male players, athletic scholarships are available if they have a UTR range of 9.5 to 13.5+ across several divisions, and the higher a player's UTR, the more opportunities will be available. The same applies to females with a UTR range of 6.5 to 10.5+.

---

12 College Scholarships, 'Tennis Scholarships For Your College Education', www.collegescholarships.org/scholarships/sports/tennis.htm

The earlier you know what your child's UTR needs to be, the better you can plan, which will increase the likelihood of your child achieving their goal in this area. In the next chapter, you will find a tracking table across every age group so that you can see what level of college your child is tracking towards.

Academic requirements

In the majority of cases, elite tennis players will get a large percentage of their college scholarship based on their tennis performances, but there are also minimum academic requirements to be eligible.

As early as Year 9 of high school, students need to understand the following academic requirements of Division 1 and 2 US colleges (there is further detail on this in the next chapter):

- Subject selection: students will need to undertake and pass sixteen core courses from Year 9 onwards, including subjects such as English, maths, science, social science, plus four additional courses.

- US grade point averages (GPA): students will need to average Bs and Cs in all of their core courses in Australia as a minimum to be eligible for most Division 1 and Division 2 programmes, which equates to an Australian grade point average of 3.5+ (converts to a 2.5 US GPA).

- Suite of Assessments tests (SAT) scores: this is a one-off exam that students will generally sit during or after Year 12. Division 1 and 2 colleges are generally looking for a minimum SAT score of 1,000. Students can re-sit this exam if they don't achieve their required score (see www.collegeboard.org).

It's important to note that if players do not meet academic requirements for Division 1 and 2, there are other options and pathways available such as junior college, which can be a stepping stone to the division your child is looking to play in. There are also hundreds of Division 3 NCAA and National Association of Intercollegiate Athletics (NAIA) programmes (smaller four-year programmes) which don't require the core course prerequisites for entry into college.

Every country will have a slightly different schooling system and you'll need to seek advice from an expert before making academic decisions.

Other requirements

Besides basic tennis and academic requirements, colleges are also looking for factors such as:

- Tennis achievements:
  - Strong doubles results as well as singles results, as this is a key component of college tennis competition

- Proof of progression in tennis results over a long period
- A well-structured and appropriate video highlighting the child's strengths and abilities

- Personal and athletic characteristics:

  - Recommendations from established, credible coaches in the form of references
  - Character references from school
  - Details of any charitable work or past activities that show good character
  - Recommendations from a credible college placement company

Mistakes to avoid

One of the hardest aspects of going to a US college is finding one that is the right fit for the individual. With around 4,500 to choose from, it's no wonder that many people run into trouble.

There are a number of mistakes that parents make when taking the application process into their own hands, including:

- Not understanding eligibility requirements from a tennis and an academic perspective. This is by far the most common mistake.

- Application mistakes. Parents have to face a huge learning curve in a short period of time, and one application mistake can cost their child a year of eligibility.

- Not understanding the subtle and ever-changing rules and restrictions of the NCAA and NAIA.

- Waiting until Year 12 for advice.

- Relying on other families who have only been through this process once. No two families will have the same process or outcome.

- Rushing the coach contact process.

- Accepting the first offer that comes to hand.

- Prioritising the wrong things, for example the college location versus the coach.

- Doing it themselves. The danger here is parents not being aware of the eligibility pitfalls, and more importantly, putting themselves in a situation where each coach is guiding them on their decision rather than an independent, unbiased expert.

Unfortunately, in recent years we have seen parents make several of these mistakes and can't recommend strongly enough that you utilise the services of a college placement expert to guide you through the process and help find the college that suits your child. The NCAA website (www.NCAA.org) is a great information source about all the different colleges and opportunities for sports scholarships.

CASE STUDY – LUKE'S OPPORTUNITY AT HARVARD

After I'd had some success and won the Australian Open junior doubles title, my phone started ringing. Many US college coaches wanted to offer me scholarships to play for their team. One of those calls came from the head coach at Harvard University. Harvard is known as one of the best universities in the world but, being young and naïve and not really understanding the significance of it, I declined the opportunity.

A big reason for my decision at that time (early 1990s) was that no one really saw college as a pathway for professional tennis players. Instead, we looked at college as a place where players went if they weren't good enough to make it on the ATP/WTA tour. I really wanted to become a professional tennis player, and the advice I received at the time was that college wouldn't be the right choice.

What I didn't realise was that if I had accepted the offer to go to Harvard I would have been on the same team as James Blake, who eventually reached a career high of world number four on the ATP tour and accumulated over US$7 million prize money. Missing the opportunity to receive an education from Harvard is one of my biggest life regrets.

Choosing a high school that balances academic studies and tennis

If you and your child are considering the pathway of a US college scholarship, the high school your child attends can have a significant impact on their ability to reach their potential as a tennis player.

In primary school (ages five to twelve), the school is less impactful as academic studies in this age group are less critical and it's relatively easy for your child to get the tennis training hours they require to become an elite player. In high school (ages twelve to eighteen), the training, competition and academic requirements all increase at the same time, so it can be one of the most challenging periods for an elite tennis player.

These are the most common challenges that players face if they and their parents have chosen an inappropriate school for pursuing elite tennis:

- As the academic requirements increase, the student decreases their training and competition load, which can severely limit tennis progress.
- For an elite player in Year 7 and 8, there are lots of older students to practise with, but by the later years in high school, these older players will have graduated. Your child could then become the best player at the school with no other students to push them.

- Students in their mid-teens are often experimenting with alcohol and recreational drugs, which can derail the focus and potential of any elite player.

It's vitally important to choose a school that balances your child's tennis and academic needs. If the school you've chosen doesn't provide a quality tennis programme, make sure there are excellent training opportunities close by that your child can attend before and/or after school.

Chapters 5 and 6 will detail guidelines on optimal training and competition loads to factor in when you're making decisions around your child's school.

The optimal high school for elite players is one that has a top-quality tennis programme with flexibility and opportunities to compete on weekends, and also provides a good level of education.

CASE STUDY – RYAN'S EXAMPLE OF CHOOSING A HIGH SCHOOL

I went to primary and high school in Forster, which is a town of around 20,000 population on the New South Wales coast of Australia. I was among the best players in my age group in Australia and had aspirations of competing on the professional tour.

While there were some really good tennis players in my home town, my parents realised I needed a stronger training environment to keep moving my game forward. They decided to look at options in Sydney for an elite tennis programme that would allow me to continue my schooling at the same time.

After extensive research, they discovered there weren't any suitable options, so they decided I'd go to the United States to the John Newcombe Tennis Academy. This allowed me to get a large amount of practice hours on court and go to school at the same time.

Having the ability to train more accelerated my tennis progress and enabled me to overtake many of my peer group who were stuck in high schools that prevented them from getting an appropriate amount of training and match play. By the end of that year I'd had some exceptionally strong tournament results and was offered a scholarship into the AIS based in Melbourne, so I transferred my schooling to distance education. Most of the best players in the world for my age group were training full time so I needed to do the same to have any hope of keeping up with the best.

CASE STUDY – LUKE'S HIGH SCHOOL EXAMPLE

I was educated at St Aloysius, which is a private school located in Sydney's Lower North Shore. Going to a school with heavy academic requirements, compulsory sport on Saturdays and limited tennis training opportunities meant I had enormous challenges when it came to getting the required hours on court.

In my first year in high school, almost every day my mother would pick me up from school, which was a forty-five-minute drive away from home, doing another forty-five-minute journey to the training venue. After I had been on court for a couple of hours, she would pick me up and drive me home.

After a while this became unsustainable for my mother. Luckily my coach at the time, Kim Warwick, offered for me to stay with his family a couple of nights each week. On the nights I stayed with Kim's family, I would finish training around 8pm, have dinner, then study until I went to sleep.

In the morning, I'd get up at first light, do some on-court training with Kim followed by physical training on the running track, then Kim's wife would drive me to catch public transport to school, which I was often late for. This meant that a lot of my weekdays involved hitting the court at 6am, going to school all day, then training on court until 8pm. At the time I was growing up in Sydney, there wasn't any other way to get the fifteen or more practice hours per week I needed to achieve my goals of becoming a professional player. I could have decided to do less, but this would have meant that I wouldn't have become good enough, so this wasn't an option for me.

Summary

Students can get a great head start in life by combining their love for tennis with a US college education, but there are many things parents need to take into consideration when their child is going down this path. In particular, they need to understand the specific requirements US colleges have.

Actions to consider:

- When choosing a high school for your child, understand how it can complement their tennis programme.

- Engage as soon as possible with somebody who has expertise and experience in helping students obtain athletic scholarships to US colleges. An example of a good consultancy is Study and Play USA, which players in our tennis academy, Voyager, have used with success.

- Pay attention to your child's UTR progress as well as their national tennis ranking. We will explore this more in Chapter 4.

- Set goals and develop a plan based on the outcome that you and your child want to achieve, which is what the next chapter is all about.

4

The Power Of Setting Goals And Measuring Progress

> You have to believe in the long-term plan you have but you need the short-term goals to motivate and inspire you.
> — Roger Federer, winner of twenty grand slams and former world number one

This chapter outlines how taking a purposely goal-oriented approach to your child's tennis development can be hugely beneficial. It also explains how you can use the UTR system as a tool to evaluate progress and benchmark where your child is compared with their peers and whether they are on track to achieve their desired goals for their tennis career. US colleges need clear benchmarks of a player's UTR and academic performance for acceptance.

At the end of the chapter is a framework for setting goals and developing an action plan.

Goal setting

> I always work with a goal – and the goal is to improve as a player and a person. That, finally, is the most important thing of all.
> — Rafael Nadal, *The Guardian*, 2009

To achieve the outcome that you and your child want for their tennis, it is critical to set goals from which you can make a plan. Developing a tennis game that enables your child to compete and win against other players at the level they desire is a long-term project that requires continual improvement, so identifying key areas and then setting specific targets is a powerful technique.

The power of goal setting is described in the compelling book *What They Don't Teach You at Harvard Business School* by Mark McCormack (who founded International Management Group Sport).[13] In his book, Mark describes a study conducted in the Harvard 1979 MBA programme. The students were asked the question, 'Have you set clear written goals for your future and made plans to accomplish them?'

---

13 M. H. McCormack, *What They Don't Teach You at Harvard Business School* (Profile Books, 2014)

THE POWER OF SETTING GOALS AND MEASURING PROGRESS

- 3% of the students had written goals with plans to achieve them
- 13% had some idea of goals, but they weren't written down
- 84% had no specific goals

Ten years later, the graduates were interviewed again. The results were incredible:

- The 13% who had goals were earning on average twice as much as the 84% who had no goals
- The 3% who had clearly defined written goals were earning an average of **ten times** more than all of their other classmates combined

Goal setting and measuring progress increase motivation and sharpen focus, so they are things many of the world's best players do regularly.

Measuring the outcome

Measuring progress is critical to top players to see whether they are on or off track to achieve their goals. When they are competing professionally, the ranking systems are a good reflection of their level.

Within junior tennis, this wasn't the case. The only way to measure progress for junior players was by looking at birth year rankings in their country.

These rankings are useful from the point of view of measuring your child's birth year ranking against competitor players, but they are blunt tools as they can be inflated by players doing well in tournaments with weak fields. As a result, you can't rely on them fully as an accurate tool for measuring progress. You definitely can't rely on them for measuring progress compared to players internationally.

The ultimate tennis measuring tool

For the first time in tennis, juniors can now measure their level against players from all over the world through the UTR. We highly recommend all elite players and parents become familiar with this as it is the best way that we've seen to track progress.

The UTR is much like the handicap system in golf and works out a player's rating based on their last thirty match performances, taking into account the number of games they've won/lost.

For players who have competed in at least thirty recorded UTR matches, the accuracy is quite amazing. Players with a relatively similar UTR – within 0.5 of a rating level – will generally have a competitive match against each other, while matches involving players with a UTR difference over 1 will tend to be one sided.

The UTR allows players to measure themselves against players at any level of the game, including the pros.

As an example, a fourteen-year-old player who has just won nationals in their country may be interested in how good they are compared to the best players in the world for their age. They can find out by looking at who won the 14/U World Championships or the 14/U European Championships (where many of the world's best juniors compete). They can then search that player's UTR and compare it to their own.

The UTR shines the spotlight on a player's real ability to play competitive matches. There are players all over the world who choose to chase points to inflate their ranking, but if they are doing so by beating easy players all the time, then it won't necessarily correlate to an improved UTR.

Players can now use their UTR as a focus for their development. As a player improves under match conditions, so will their UTR. It's also an incredible tool for tracking progress.

Voyager player tracking model

To produce the player model, we used a combination of the UTR, National, International Tennis Federation (ITF), ATP and WTA rankings systems and US college data so that you can see what level your child is currently tracking for at each age group. There are a few things to keep in mind when you're viewing the model:

1. Every player will develop physically and mentally at different ages. From our experience, players who have a late growth spurt will experience a climb in their UTR in line with this.

2. Players who are looking to go to college but are young for the year at school will need to prioritise their year before their age when looking at the tracking table. This is because players will be accepted into a college within a couple of months of completing Year 12.

3. If your child is not tracking where you'd like, don't worry. The research in Chapters 5 and 6 will provide an analysis of the right quantity of training and matches to achieve the various levels of tennis.

4. Please take into account that these are estimations based on what's happening in August 2019. These benchmarks are likely to change slightly year to year with periodic updates to these graphs available on our website voyagertennis.com/blog if changes are to occur.

The levels in the following table represent the opportunities that will be available and most suitable to your child if they are tracking in that area.

THE POWER OF SETTING GOALS AND MEASURING PROGRESS

	Level 1
National position	These players are typically among the best few players in their country for their age group.
US college opportunities	Tennis scholarships into most prestigious US college teams, including Ivy League

Playing opportunities	• National and international competitions
	  – National ranking tournaments (usually winning or making finals for their age group)
	  – Junior World Championships (Orange Bowl/Tarbes)
	  – ITF Junior World Circuit (if prepared to sacrifice education and travel extensively)
	• Representative tennis
	  – Area representation (country representation)
	• Club tennis and tours
	  – European club tennis (potential to be paid well for every match)
	  – Professional ATP/WTA tour (top 100 in the world possible)
	  – Seniors tour (likely highly world ranked for age groups)

	Level 2
National position	These players are typically good nationally ranked players who are around the fringe of gaining acceptance into closed national title junior events in their respective countries.
US college opportunities	Tennis scholarships into good Division 1 colleges

Playing opportunities	• National competitions
	  – Local inter-club tennis (competing against other teams in area)
	  – Inter-school tennis competitions
	  – National ranking tournaments
	• Representative tennis
	  – Area representation (local or state representation)
	• Club tennis and tours
	  – European club tennis (payment likely to represent a team)
	  – Professional ATP/WTA tour (lower and mid-level professional possible)
	  – Seniors' tour

	Level 3
National position	These players often start a committed training and competition schedule later than level 1 and 2 players. They are good junior players who play number 1 or 2 for their high school.
US college opportunities	Tennis scholarships into Division 2, junior colleges and below

Continued

Playing Some common and suitable opportunities for
opportunities these players are:

- National competitions
  - Local inter-club tennis (competing against other teams in area)
  - Inter-school tennis competitions (often playing number 1 or 2 for school team)
  - National ranking tournaments (lower tiered events most suitable)
- Representative tennis
  - Area representation (local or regional)
- Club tennis and tours
  - Seniors' tour (will compete well in local senior tour events)

Male tennis players' UTR tracking

Age/Year at school	Level 1	Level 2	Level 3
Age 8/Year 2	3+	N/A	N/A
Age 9/Year 3	5+	3+	N/A
Age 10/Year 4	6.25+	4+	3.25+
Age 11/Year 5	7.5+	5.25+	4.25+
Age 12/Year 6	8.5+	6.25+	5.5+
Age 13/Year 7	9.5+	7.25+	6+
Age 14/Year 8	10.25+	8.25+	7+
Age 15/Year 9	11.25+	9.25+	7.75+
Age 16/Year 10	12+	10+	8.5+
Age 17/Year 11	12.75+	10.75+	9+
Age 18/Year 12	13.5+	11.5+	9.5+

Female tennis players' UTR tracking

Age/Year at school	Level 1	Level 2	Level 3
Age 8/Year 2	X	X	X
Age 9/Year 3	2.25	X	X
Age 10/Year 4	4.25+	2.5+	1.5+
Age 11/Year 5	5.75+	3.5+	2+
Age 12/Year 6	6.5+	4.75+	3+
Age 13/Year 7	7.5+	5.75	4+
Age 14/Year 8	8.75+	6.5+	4.5+
Age 15/Year 9	9.25+	7+	5+
Age 16/Year 10	9.75+	7.5+	5.5+
Age 17/Year 11	10.25+	8+	6+
Age 18/Year 12	10.5+	8.5+	6.5+

As an example, if John is in Year 9, turns fifteen this year and has a UTR of 9, he is on track to have a UTR of above 9.25 by the end of the year and to target a Division 1 college by the end of Year 12. If Bobby, who is thirteen, has the goal of a Division 1 college and has a UTR of 6, then he is way off the target of 7.25 and needs to look to adjust his training volume and match-play quantity accordingly to accelerate his UTR.

We have undertaken over 100 case studies, and some important notes and observations we have made are:

- The most common reason for a player not tracking where they'd like to be is lack of training and match play.

- Players can catch up by implementing an appropriate training and competition plan that aligns with the level of play they desire to compete at (see Chapters 5 and 6).

- With the right training and competition plan, players can jump up two UTR levels in a twelve-month period. We have seen several examples of this happening.

If you don't know what your child's UTR is, visit www.myutr.com and sign up to the premium version to get two decimal places in the rating.

Academic benchmarks

As of early 2019, these are the approximate academic benchmarks required for US colleges.

College type	Required grades from Year 10 onwards	SAT score
Ivy League and a selection of programmes from NCAA Division 1, 2 and 3	As only	1,350+
NCAA Division 1	Bs and Cs	1,000+
NCAA Division 2	Bs and Cs	1,000+
NCAA Division 3	Bs and Cs	Subject to each university
NAIA	Bs and Cs	900+
Junior college	A completed high school certificate	No specific requirements

A few points to note:

- There are exceptions to these benchmarks
- These are guidelines only and will vary in each country
- These benchmarks could change from time to time
- Subject selection is also critical for entry into US colleges

We would encourage you to seek expert advice before making big academic decisions.

For those parents looking to send their child to a university outside of the United States, there will be minimum academic requirements to reach as well. The most important aspect about setting academic goals is to know what your child wants to achieve and measure progress along the way.

Developing goals and an action plan for your child

Below is a template that players can use to set their main tennis and academic goals. We use the tennis and academic benchmarking tools in this chapter to provide players with a reference point; with regard to training hours and match-play quantity, please use the tables in the following two chapters for guidance.

THE POWER OF SETTING GOALS AND MEASURING PROGRESS

The template is self-explanatory, but it's often a useful exercise to have a session with an expert to develop the action plan.

Voyager goal setting for winning on and off the course

Note: this goal setting template is available for download from voyagertennis.com/blog

Ambitions	
Long-term goal as a player:	
Long-term career goal after tennis:	
Current school grade average:	School grade average goal:
Current UTR:	My current UTR is tracking for which level:
End of year UTR goal:	Year 12 graduation UTR goal:

Actions	
Below is a list of actions that I will be taking in order to achieve my goals	
What will I need to do to achieve my school grade goals?	
Number of hours I need to practise per week to achieve my tennis goals:	Number of matches I need to play in the next twelve months to achieve my goals:
Technical:	
Tactical:	
Psychological:	
Physical:	
Nutrition:	

Summary

Setting goals and measuring progress is an essential part of the elite player's journey. High performers across all industries are goal oriented and continually assess how they are progressing, and the UTR is a key tool for setting your child's tennis goals.

Actions to consider:

- Think about the outcomes you and your child want to achieve. What level are you aspiring to?
- Benchmark the UTR that your child needs to achieve for that level.
- Understand the academic requirements of colleges.
- Download and populate the 'actions' section of the 'goal setting for winning on and off the court' template in this chapter.

The next two chapters will help you to create a specific action plan that aligns with the goals you and your child have.

SECTION TWO
DEVELOPING A WINNING TENNIS GAME

The glory is not winning here or winning there. The glory is enjoying practising, enjoy every day, enjoying to work hard, trying to be a better player than before.
— Rafael Nadal, Twitter, US Open, 2018

5
Training

> Luck has nothing to do with it, because I have spent many, many hours, countless hours, on the court working for my one moment in time, not knowing when it would come.
> — Serena Williams, *NewsMail*, 2017

In any achievement in life, the higher the goal, the more commitment it will take. This certainly applies to tennis. Every player who reaches the highest level of the game has had to put in significant time on and off the court.

Less ambitious goals require lower levels of commitment, but commitment nonetheless. This chapter outlines training plans we recommend for players aspiring to different levels.

Hours on the court are the key to success

> Nothing can substitute for just plain hard work...
> But I was completely committed to working out to prove to myself that I still could do it.
> — Andre Agassi, *Open*, 2010

In 1993 Anders Ericsson developed the theory that it takes around 10,000 hours of deliberate practice to become world class in any field. His underlying message from over thirty years of research in this area is that talent doesn't matter – purposeful practice does.

You may be familiar with a book called *Bounce: The Myth of Talent and the Power of Practice* by Matthew Syed. This book compiles research across many areas of expertise, such as grand chess masters, athletes, musicians and artists, to understand what it takes to become world class in any field, sharing countless examples of top performers who seem to be gifted from an early age. This is actually often because they have been given extra tuition at home by their parents and have clocked up thousands of hours of practice. Examples include Tiger Woods who had hit thousands of golf balls before the age of two, Mozart who had done 3,500 hours of piano practice by the age of six, and Andre Agassi who was hitting one million balls per year as a junior. [14]

---

14 M. Syed, *Bounce: The Myth of Talent and the Power of Practice* (New York: HarperCollins, 2010)

While these examples may be extreme, the principle is that elite tennis players need thousands of quality hours on court to build up the fitness and skills to compete at a high level. Simply put, the more hours they put in on court, the better they will become.

Any parents looking to learn more on this subject, we'd strongly recommend you read *Bounce*, along with *The Talent Code* by Daniel Coyle and *Outliers* by Malcolm Gladwell.

Evidence from tennis players

Rather than provide recommendations based on guesswork or personal experiences, we conducted extensive research into how much time on court a player needs to reach the various levels of the game. We surveyed over 100 current and former players, from unranked to world number one juniors, right the way through to current and former professionals, to find out their training and match-play history up to the age of eighteen. The years leading up to eighteen are critical as players are choosing whether to take the college or professional pathway.

What we wanted to find out was:

- The player's age
- How many hours' training they did on court at each age, from starting right the way up to eighteen (if they were eighteen or older)

- How many matches they had competed in to that point
- Their playing level (ranking or rating) at that point

The findings were fascinating and remarkably consistent. We summarise them below.

The more training hours and matches they took part in, the higher the player's level. We didn't see any exceptions to this rule. Every player who put a large amount of hours into training played matches at a significantly higher level than those who didn't. There were also *no examples of players* who had put in significant hours on the court but didn't have a correspondingly high playing level.

Playing a high volume of competitive matches was the *strongest* determinant of what level a player would be playing at (we will address match-play quantities in the next chapter). Players who only played a relatively small number of matches didn't play at a high level, despite in some cases having a good training schedule.

Here are four real examples of twelve-year-old boys.

TRAINING

12/U world champion	12/U top 3 Australian ranked	12/U top 100 Australian ranked	12/U unranked player
Training hours per week, 42 weeks a year	Training hours per week, 42 weeks a year	Training hours per week, 42 weeks a year	Training hours per week, 42 weeks a year
Age 3: hours p/week: 0	Age 3: hours p/week: 0	Age 3: hours p/week: 0	Age 3: hours p/week: 0
Age 4: hours p/week: 0	Age 4: hours p/week: 0	Age 4: hours p/week: 0	Age 4: hours p/week: 0
Age 5: hours p/week: 5	Age 5: hours p/week: 3.5	Age 5: hours p/week: 0	Age 5: hours p/week: 0
Age 6: hours p/week: 10	Age 6: hours p/week: 8	Age 6: hours p/week: 0	Age 6: hours p/week: 1
Age 7: hours p/week: 15	Age 7: hours p/week: 9	Age 7: hours p/week: 0	Age 7: hours p/week: 1
Age 8: hours p/week: 15	Age 8: hours p/week: 10	Age 8: hours p/week: 1	Age 8: hours p/week: 2
Age 9: hours p/week: 15	Age 9: hours p/week: 11	Age 9: hours p/week: 4	Age 9: hours p/week: 2
Age 10: hours p/week: 15	Age 10: hours p/week: 12	Age 10: hours p/week: 6	Age 10: hours p/week: 2.5
Age 11: hours p/week: 20	Age 11: hours p/week: 12	Age 11: hours p/week: 7	Age 11: hours p/week: 2.5
Age 12: hours p/week: 20	Age 12: hours p/week: 12	Age 12: hours p/week: 8	Age 12: hours p/week: 2.5
Total training hours 4,830	Total training hours 3,255	Total training hours 1,092	Total training hours 567
+ 650 matches played (x 1.5 hours per match)	+ 760 matches played (x 1.5 hours per match)	+ 220 matches played (x 1.5 hours per match)	+ 90 matches played (x 1.5 hours per match)
Total hours on court 5,805	Total hours on court 4,395	Total hours on court 1,422	Total hours on court 702
Approx. UTR 10.75	Approx. UTR 9.6	Approx. UTR 5.1	Approx. UTR 3.6

As you can see, there is a direct correlation between the amount of hours a player spends on court and the level of the player, and this was consistent across all case studies.

Training volume

From the training history of the players we researched, here are the estimated number of training hours on court required to reach certain levels of the game. The hours per week are multiplied by forty-two as this is the average number of weeks that our students train per year. The remaining weeks are typically dedicated to tournament play or time off.

The most important column to pay attention to is the hours per week/total. From our research, this is the critical factor that determines how good a player becomes. The levels refer to those we outlined in Chapter 4.

Training hours

Benchmarking male players

Levels	Level 1		Level 2		Level 3	
Age/Year at school	P/week	Total	P/week	Total	P/week	Total
Age 5	5	210	0	0	0	0
Age 6/Kindergarten	6	462	4	168	0	0
Age 7/Year 1	7	756	5	378	4	168
Age 8/Year 2	8	1,092	6	630	5	378
Age 9/Year 3	9	1,470	7	924	6	630
Age 10/Year 4	10	1,890	8	1,260	7	924
Age 11/Year 5	11	2,352	9	1,638	7	1,218
Age 12/Year 6	12	2,856	10	2,058	8	1,554
Age 13/Year 7	13	3,402	11	2,520	8	1,890
Age 14/Year 8	14	3,990	12	3,024	8	2,226
Age 15/Year 9	14	4,578	12	3,528	9	2,604
Age 16/Year 10	15	5,208	12	4,032	9	2,982
Age 17/Year 11	16	5,880	13	4,578	10	3,402
Age 18/Year 12	16	6,552	14	5,166	10	3,822

Benchmarking female players

Levels	Level 1		Level 2		Level 3	
Age/Year at school	P/week	Total	P/week	Total	P/week	Total
Age 5	5	210	0	0	0	0
Age 6/Kindergarten	6	462	3	126	0	0
Age 7/Year 1	7	756	4	294	2	84
Age 8/Year 2	8	1,092	5	504	3	210
Age 9/Year 3	9	1,470	6	756	4	378
Age 10/Year 4	10	1,890	7	1,050	5	588
Age 11/Year 5	11	2,352	8	1,386	6	840
Age 12/Year 6	12	2,856	8	1,722	6	1,092
Age 13/Year 7	13	3,402	9	2,100	7	1,386
Age 14/ Year 8	14	3,990	10	2,520	8	1,722
Age 15/Year 9	14	4,578	11	2,982	8	2,058
Age 16/Year 10	15	5,208	12	3,486	9	2,436
Age 17/Year 11	15	5,838	13	4,032	10	2,856
Age 18/Year 12	16	6,510	14	4,620	10	3,276

Our research shows that female players who are pursuing college tennis need to do less than male players to achieve the same level. This is likely to be for two reasons:

1. There are fewer females playing competitive tennis than males, so less competition.

2. Female players have more US college scholarships available than male players, depending on what

division of college tennis a player is competing at. Generally female players have eight full athletic scholarships per team while male players have 4.5 scholarships per team.

Choosing a training environment

One of the factors that Matthew Syed calls a key determinant of successful athletes is that the 10,000 hours of practice need to be *purposeful*.[15] It is not enough to just hit balls; you need a plan, intent, purpose behind how your child trains to ensure that those hours are as productive as possible. Choosing the right training environment is paramount.

For aspiring elite players, there are a number of factors to look for when you're choosing a training environment:

- A programme that covers all facets of an elite player's development
- Specialist high-performance coaches
- Other elite players to train and play matches against
- Guidance to players and parents from experts who understand the journey
- An enjoyable experience

---

15 M. Syed, *Bounce: The Myth of Talent and the Power of Practice* (New York: HarperCollins, 2010)

Developing a balanced training programme

Practice. A good elite-player programme will have some great opportunities for practising, usually in a high-intensity squad format where players are pushed by the coaches and their peers to work hard and develop all areas of their game.

Match play. As match play is critical to the development of each player, a good programme will provide the opportunities for regular match play against other players in the programme who are at a similar level. This match play is in addition to tournaments.

Sports psychology. Tennis is one of the most mentally challenging sports when it comes to competing under intense individual pressure. Players need access to good sports psychology to provide them with strategies on how to deal with these mental challenges.

Physical development. A high-quality programme will either provide the physical development aspect or refer you on to specialist trainers in this area. The number one priority is injury prevention. To achieve great things in tennis, your child needs to be able to spend a lot of time on court. Repetitive injuries can sideline players, sometimes for months at a time, which will halt progress significantly. Every elite player needs to work through a weekly injury-prevention programme set by a professional. Only once this is in place can players work on other physical development areas such as speed, endurance, power, core stability and flexibility.

Nutrition. Your child's body is essentially a vehicle, and if they put the wrong fuel in it, it won't work well. Good nutrition can make a huge difference to energy and how well your child will play, so guidance as part of the programme is essential.

Parent education. Parents are by far the biggest influence on their child's success (even more than the coach). The programme needs to provide them with an understanding of what best-practice tennis parenting looks like.

The coaching team. There is a huge difference between a club coach and a high-performance coach. A high-performance coach is somebody who specialises in working with elite players and will ideally have played at a high level, had years of coaching experience, and be a great role model for the students by encouraging the development of their games and positive personal qualities. The high-performance coach will be able to provide structured programmes not just for one session, but over the medium-term training blocks and long-term (yearly) in accordance with the player's goals.

The players. A high-quality training environment will consist of players who are all looking to become the best they can be. Being in an environment where there are a lot of players working hard towards similar goals is motivating and can make hard work seem easy. In an ideal world, there will be a group of players around your child's level, and it's a bonus if there are players who are better.

Guidance. As the elite-player journey is complex and difficult for parents to navigate at times, it is important that you have guidance along the way. This will either be included in the programme or you'll have access to coaches who can answer various questions about how to give your child every chance of success.

Creating a training plan

Before considering a weekly training plan, first ask yourself these two questions using the UTR tracking table in Chapter 4:

1. What are my child's goals in tennis?
2. Are they on or off track for achieving them?

The answers to these questions will determine the action plan you and your child need and what their weekly training plan will look like. If your child is not tracking well for their goals, use the training and match-play guidelines in this chapter to establish what volume of each your child is going to need to get back on track.

TRAINING

Example of a training plan

A twelve-year-old female player who is going to school full time and looking to play Division 1 college tennis on a full scholarship has looked at the suggested training hours for their age and realised that they should be training around eight hours per week on court. The weekly schedule could look something like this:

12-YEAR-OLD: WEEKLY SCHEDULE							
Time	Monday	Tuesday	Wednesday	Thursday	Friday	Saturday	Sunday
7am		Private Lesson			Athletic Development		
7:30am							
8am							
8:30am	School	School	School	School	School		
9am	School	School	School	School	School		
9:30am	School	School	School	School	School		
10am	School	School	School	School	School	Time for other sports or activities or tennis tournaments	Time for other sports or activities or tennis tournaments
10:30am	School	School	School	School	School		
11am	School	School	School	School	School		
11:30am	School	School	School	School	School		
12pm	School	School	School	School	School		
12:30pm	School	School	School	School	School		
1pm	School	School	School	School	School		
1:30pm	School	School	School	School	School		
2pm	School	School	School	School	School		
2:30pm	School	School	School	School	School		
3pm	School	School	School	School	School		
3:30pm							
4pm	Time for other sports or activities such as music or extra study	Organised Practice Session	Homework	Homework	Organised Practice Match		
4:30pm							
5pm							
5:30pm							
6pm							
6:30pm			Performance Squad	Performance Squad			
7pm							
7:30pm							

Figure 5.1 An example of a weekly schedule

Many players who attend a typical school full time will max out on eight to ten hours' practice per week as there simply isn't any more free time. This will depend on where a player lives and the amount of training opportunities in close proximity to them. But eight to ten hours' training per week through high school will often produce a deficit in the hours an elite player requires on court. The best way to make up for this is by ensuring your child plays a high volume of matches, which can include weekly junior and adult competitions and more tournament play (see Chapter 6 for match-play quantity guidelines).

Players in primary school typically have no trouble with achieving the training and match-play hours they require. The challenge occurs once players reach high school when tennis and academic requirements increase at the same time. If you are struggling with this balance, look for tennis schools that combine tennis and academic studies together. Most big cities around the world will have a couple of options for your child.

Summary

The number of hours your child spends on court is a vital element in achieving the outcomes they desire. The UTR benchmarking tool is a good means of evaluating how many training hours your child should be putting in. It is also important to consider the training

TRAINING

environment to make sure each hour is as beneficial as possible.

Actions to consider:

- Assess where you child is currently tracking.

- Decide on what your child's goals are, what level they want to achieve.

- Create a weekly training plan with an expert that delivers the training volume your child needs in an environment that is purposeful and conducive to them achieving their goals.

- Develop a weekly training plan alongside a match-play plan.

6
Match-Play Quantity

> Losses have propelled me to even bigger places, so I understand the importance of losing. You can never get complacent because a loss is always around the corner.
> — Venus Williams, former world number one and winner of seven grand slams, *USA Today*, 2010

Playing a high volume of competitive matches is one of the most beneficial things a player can do to develop their game, their ranking and their UTR. Our case studies and database show that match-play quantity is the strongest determinant of the level that a player reaches. Without exception, the best players in any country have a high match count.

This chapter outlines the benefits of match play to a tennis player; match-play quantities dependent on the level your child is targeting; the variety of opportunities available to access competitive match play; the importance of maximising the learning and development from each match; and how to prepare for a match by adapting to the conditions.

The benefits of match play

Match play is a key means for a player to develop their game, and playing matches against opponents of a similar level is the best way to accelerate their development. The more competitive matches a player can play, the better match player they become. The reasons for this are:

- Tactically, players become more intelligent and pick up on common patterns that opponents use, reading the play earlier and earlier over time.

- Physically, players' bodies become accustomed to the intensity, rhythm and duration of competitive matches. Over time, they build up a strong tolerance to deal with all of the physical demands of tennis.

- Mentally, players become accustomed to handling the ups and downs of matches and high-pressure situations. Players who don't compete tend to panic and play the big points poorly, while experienced match players stay more composed and execute more effectively under pressure.

- Intensive practice of key shots in tennis – the serve and return. Statistically *70% of all points are won/lost in the first four shots*, making the serve and return the most important strokes to develop, but often training sessions don't devote a lot of time to the serve and return. The players with a high match count become skilled in the first four shots of each point, but the *vast majority* of tennis players and parents don't realise this.

Match-play scheduling

There are a number of critical factors when it comes to producing a successful schedule for your child:

- Planning the appropriate number of matches for your child's goals. Knowing how many matches they need to play each year will influence how many tournaments and match-play opportunities you'll need to be pursuing.

- Win/loss ratio. Perhaps the most important factor in developing your child's tournament schedule is adjusting it constantly to ensure they have a win/loss ratio above 50%. Ideally, strive to put together a tournament schedule for your child that provides them with an average of two wins to one loss. As a general rule, if a player has been on a winning streak, it is time for them to play up and compete in more challenging tournaments. On the flip side, if a player has taken a series of losses in a row, look at match-play options where the competition is not as strong. There is generally nothing worse for a player's confidence than to take a number of consecutive losses, so from a parent's perspective, you need to keep an eye out for this and take action as soon as you see it happening.

- Complementing tournament play with competitive matches from a number of different sources.

- Seeking tournaments in conditions that suit your child's game style.

Doubles is crucial in developing match-play skills

A lot of parents and players overlook the importance of doubles and just play singles at tournaments. Doubles has a lot of benefits, such as:

- Improving adjustment skills considerably due to the quick exchanges and reflexes required.

- Giving a great opportunity to get experienced at the net. A lot of junior players have a strong baseline game, but don't come to the net often. Doubles is a great way to counteract this.

- It is all about serve and return and first shot, which relates well to singles.

- Giving players more experience in playing under pressure. In doubles, particularly at a high level, there are many tie breakers and tight matches.

- Experiencing tennis as a team sport. This can be a lot of fun as your child shares the highs and lows with a teammate.

- It can be a great confidence booster as your child can often beat players in doubles that they may not have beaten in singles, which can help them win more singles matches.

We strongly suggest that players always enter doubles at tournaments. Make sure your child finds a partner that they combine well with and enjoy spending time with.

CASE STUDY – RYAN'S EXPERIENCE IN DOUBLES

Doubles was a part of tennis that I always enjoyed and excelled in. It was great for my all-court game style and improved my serve, return and net play enormously, which benefitted my singles game.

Doubles also played a big part in building my confidence. While my career-high world junior singles rankings was sixteen, I managed to achieve the number one in the world junior ranking in doubles. Through the doubles events, I enjoyed wins over some of the world's best singles players, including Jo-Wilfried Tsonga, Tomáš Berdych and Robin Söderling. It was a big confidence booster to beat players like this, even if it was in doubles.

Target match-play quantities

Below are the average match-play counts of all the case studies we conducted. The most important column is match-play quantity to date. This is how a player can determine if they are on track with the level they are targeting or need to catch up.

The levels refer to those we outlined in Chapter 4.

Benchmarking male players

Levels	Level 1		Level 2		Level 3	
Age/Year at school	P/year	Total	P/year	Total	P/year	Total
Age 7/Year 1	60	60	0	0	0	0
Age 8/Year 2	65	125	45	45	0	0
Age 9/Year 3	65	190	50	95	35	35
Age 10/Year 4	85	275	60	155	40	75
Age 11/Year 5	95	370	70	225	45	120
Age 12/Year 6	110	480	75	300	50	170
Age 13/Year 7	110	590	80	380	55	225
Age 14/Year 8	110	700	85	465	60	285
Age 15/Year 9	120	820	90	555	60	345
Age 16/Year 10	120	940	95	650	65	410
Age 17/Year 11	120	1,060	100	750	65	475
Age 18/Year 12	120	1,180	100	850	65	540

MATCH-PLAY QUANTITY

Benchmarking female players

Levels	Level 1		Level 2		Level 3	
Age/Year at school	P/year	Total	P/year	Total	P/year	Total
Age 7/Year 1	60	60	0	0	0	0
Age 8/Year 2	65	125	30	30	0	0
Age 9/Year 3	65	190	35	65	30	30
Age 10/Year 4	80	270	45	110	35	65
Age 11/Year 5	90	360	50	160	40	105
Age 12/Year 6	100	460	55	215	40	145
Age 13/Year 7	100	560	60	275	45	190
Age 14/Year 8	100	660	65	340	45	235
Age 15 /Year 9	110	770	65	405	50	285
Age 16/Year 10	120	890	70	475	55	340
Age 17/Year 11	120	1,010	75	550	55	395
Age 18/Year 12	120	1,130	80	630	60	455

For example, the top three players, average in each birth year for boys and girls, as of November 2018 have played the followed number of Australian ranking matches:

	Boys' match count	Girls' match count
Tenth birth year	293	287
Eleventh birth year	367	300
Twelfth birth year	616	380
Thirteenth birth year	540	442
Fourteenth birth year	568	589
Fifteenth birth year	728	715

A couple of notes:

- These are just Australian ranking tournament matches. These players generally would have played the equivalent of 50–100 matches or more outside of Australian ranking tournaments, such as weekly competitions, team events and junior round-robin tournaments.
- We didn't include age sixteen and onwards as the top three players in that birth year are playing fewer national events and more ITF and futures etc.

Competitive opportunities

Tennis has a range of team and individual competitive opportunities available for players all around the world. Not many people are aware of all these opportunities, so we have listed some of the most common.

For juniors

Local inter-club tennis. Inter-club tennis is common in a lot of cities/communities around the world. This is where junior and adult players are placed into teams to represent a particular tennis club and compete against teams from other clubs. Inter-club competitions usually start at an intermediate junior level and go right the way up to the best adult players in the area. This can be a great way for your child to compete alongside friends in a competitive environment.

Inter-school tennis. A lot of strong tennis nations have a good inter-school tennis competition structure. This is where players represent their school and compete against others in a team format. Competition against other schools usually starts locally, then it takes place nationally and finally goes all the way to the world championships.

The world school tennis championships is run by the International School Sport Federation and is usually hosted in Europe.

National ranking tournaments. These are where many of the best junior players from each country compete. The draws are usually a knockout format and players who advance the furthest in the draw accumulate the most amount of points, which improves a player's national ranking.

Players who compete in junior ranking events have more of an individual focus and can usually enter both singles and doubles events. National selectors often choose which players to invite into representative teams and subsidised state and national programmes based on their results from junior events.

In most countries, there are national ranking open events for all age groups.

UTR match-play events. These events are typically for players of all ages, genders and abilities, and aim to provide participants with a number of highly competitive matches. This is done by grouping players together with those of a similar rating to play a guaranteed number of matches. UTR match-play events are not based on age groups or gender, with only a player's rating determining which group they will compete against. As a result, players who compete in these events often play against people they have never played before (cross-gender and age group matches are common), with matches generally being a lot closer than in regular tournament play.

Junior world championships. For players who are doing well in their country and would like to see how they compare on the world stage, there are junior world championships. The official event called the Orange Bowl is based in Florida each year and starts from the 12/U age group through to the 18/U.

In Europe, there is a tournament called Tarbes, which is held in France and is commonly regarded as the unofficial junior world championships. This event also has most of the best junior players in Europe and around the world competing in it.

Area representation (region/state/country). These are competitions involving players representing their local area, region, state or country. Formats are for juniors and open players with the pinnacles for juniors being the World Youth Cup, in which the best juniors from each country compete against each other, or the Davis and Fed Cup open events, where the top professionals from each country compete against each other. The Davis and Fed Cup formats will change from 2019/2020, but the concept of players representing their country will remain the same.

ITF world junior circuit. This provides a series of world ranking tournaments with several tiers of events, which start from Grade 5 right the way through to the junior grand slams in which the best juniors in the world compete. As of 2019, the top junior players in the world will receive qualifying and main draw entry into certain levels of pro-tour events.

For adults

College/university tennis. This is where players represent their university in a team-event format. There are various versions of this around the world, but by far the biggest competition between universities is in the United States. There, players from all around the world are offered full or partial tennis scholarships to play for a college.

This is where many of the world's best eighteen to twenty-two-year-olds are competing and is now the most common pathway to the professional tour. It's also a great way to receive a free or heavily subsidised college education (see Chapter 3 for more detail).

Professional. The professional tour is the pinnacle of tennis and has several tiers of tournaments designed for players to work their way up to competing in the grand slams (see Chapter 13 for more detail).

Europe club tennis. Club tennis in Europe is popular among elite players, from US college level to ATP/WTA professionals. Competitions are played between clubs in Europe, typically over a six- to eight-week period in countries such as Germany, France, Italy and Sweden.

Club matches are often funded by wealthy businesspeople who take a lot of pride in their club being successful. Players are typically paid anywhere from 100 euros per match to 20,000 euros per match for the top 100 ATP/WTA players. Players from foreign countries will usually get accommodation and flights included as well.

Many professionals and college players participate in European club tennis as a way to increase their bank balances and have a base to train at in Europe.

Preparing for match play

To maximise your child's chances of success and getting the most out of each match, there are three key things to make sure they do: understand the match conditions, develop a structured game plan based on their strengths, and conduct a debrief post-match to ensure they take key learnings from the match. We will explain the second and third of these in detail in Chapter 8.

Understanding match conditions

Most junior players and their parents don't understand how big an impact playing conditions can have on the performances of each player under match conditions. This is particularly important when players are older and have a clearly developed game style. For players in younger age groups, it has less of an impact. Young players need to compete on all surfaces and in all conditions for their development.

Over time, a player can get an understanding of what conditions are more suitable for them and seek suitable playing conditions that will increase their chances of playing at their best.

CASE STUDY - RYAN'S EXPERIENCE

I started playing professional events at the age of fifteen and was initially surprised by the level of detail that professional players focused on. A lot of players talked about things I'd never really considered. Almost all of the talk at junior tournaments had been around which players had entered in tournaments and their strengths and weaknesses. The professional players still had a focus on the players, but they placed far more emphasis on adapting to and using the playing conditions to gain an advantage over an opponent. They were interested in things like what balls were being used, how the courts were bouncing, what footwear to use on clay or grass, and what string tension to use if the weather was either hot or cold. Players new to the pro tour would often be blissfully unaware of many of these crucial factors of match performance, which made success at this level a lot more difficult for them.

Factors that affect match conditions

There are a number of factors that impact match conditions, such as tennis balls, the court surface, the weather conditions and altitude.

Tennis balls

Tennis balls often have the biggest influence on the match conditions, yet a lot of junior players don't even know what ball they are using. Players can fall into the trap of thinking all balls are the same, but this couldn't be further from the truth. Tennis balls vary quite a lot in size, bounce, weight and durability, which can alter how the ball behaves during a match.

The ITF oversees the official ball for all professional events and has an acceptable range of size and weight, allowing for variances from ball to ball. According to ITF standards, tennis balls must measure from 2.57 to

2.70 inches in diameter and weigh between 1.975 and 2.095 ounces. Considering this range of variability in tennis balls used by professionals, you can imagine how big the differences are for junior events.

'It is funny that balls are not spoken about, but they have a massive impact on a tournament and a player… The first thing we do when we get to the tournament is work out what tension [the racquet] will be with that ball.'[16]
— David Taylor, who coached Sam Stosur (former US Open champion)

The type of balls used at tournaments can have a dramatic effect on the playing conditions. As an example, players who like to be aggressive and finish the point off early will be far more suited to a quicker ball and find it more challenging to compete with a slower ball. There are many different types of balls and it's important to be aware of the effect they have on the playing conditions.

Tennis court surfaces

Some common tournament playing surfaces are hardcourt, clay, synthetic grass and natural grass, which will impact the effectiveness of a player's game dramatically. And even if a player decides to play on just

---

16 Tim Newcomb, 'Beyond the Bounce', *Sports Illustrated* (2015) www.si.com/tennis/2015/10/14/tennis-balls-atp-wta-matches

one surface, eg hardcourt, the way every court plays is completely different. As an example, the bounce on a hardcourt can be fast or slow, low or high. Surface can have a huge impact on how well your child plays.

You'll probably have noticed certain pros performing really well at particular grand slams each year. For example, Rafael Nadal's game is most suited to slow, high-bouncing clay courts, which is why he's been so successful at the French Open, while Roger Federer prefers the faster, lower bouncing grass courts at Wimbledon.

Here are some common characteristics of the main court surfaces and the game styles that are most suitable to each.

Hardcourt

Bounce. Hardcourts have a true and predictable bounce. They can be anything from low to high bouncing.

Speed. This can vary from slow to fast.

Players' movement. This surface suits standard movement with generally no sliding.

Suited game style. Fast hardcourts that have a low bounce will suit aggressive baseliners and all-court players who generally hit the ball flatter. A slow, high-bouncing hardcourt can suit players who are patient and play with more spin on the ball. A medium-paced court with a medium bounce is generally a great leveller for all players with no specific advantage going to any one playing style.

In recent years, the Australian Open has probably been the best example of a grand slam with a neutral playing surface each year.

Clay court

Bounce. Sometimes a clay court is uneven if it's not groomed well and the ball can skid off the lines. It often has higher than the average bounce. The ball tends to grip the court, which increases the effectiveness of topspin on groundstrokes and serve.

Speed. It is generally slow, particularly if courts have been recently watered. The dryer the court, the faster it becomes.

Players' movement. This surface requires different movement patterns from hardcourts, the biggest difference being that players need to learn to slide into the ball and not after it. Players who use hardcourt footwork on clay tend to slide after the shot, losing 1–2 metres every shot which makes them a lot less effective on this surface.

Suited game style. Due to the typically slow, high-bouncing court, this surface suits players who use moderate to heavy topspin, are patient and consistent, and know how to slide into the ball. The all-court aggressive players tend not to be as effective on this surface as it's more difficult to hit winners and get cheap points.

Grass court

Bounce. This is generally low. Due to the uneven surface on a lot of grass courts, the bounce can be random, which requires players to adjust.

Speed. Generally fast – although how the grass is laid can determine the speed of the court.

Players' movement. Standard hardcourt movement works due to players not being able to slide, but players will need to set their centre of gravity lower than they would normally because of the low-bouncing nature of the court.

Suited game style. Aggressive baseliners who hit the ball flatter and lower than other court players; all-court players who like to take the ball early and attack; big servers; serve-volleyers; and players who like to play first-strike tennis.

Synthetic grass court

Bounce. On this court bounce is typically low. The ball can skid off the court, particularly when the surface is wet.

Speed. This depends on each individual court, but typically the wetter synthetic grass courts are, the faster they get. This is the opposite to clay.

Players' movement. Synthetic grass courts with the standard amount of sand will require players to slide to the ball (similar to clay court movement), while courts without much sand will require hardcourt movement.

Suited game style. Crafty players who enjoy using the slice; aggressive baseliners who hit the ball flatter and lower; all-court players who like to take the ball early and attack; big servers; serve-volleyers; and players who like to play first-strike tennis. Counterpunchers who like playing patiently with heavy topspin will usually underperform on this surface.

The weather conditions

Temperature. Some players handle the heat better than others. Generally fitter players perform better in hot conditions as it takes more energy than usual to produce the same output.

Hotter temperatures also produce fast playing conditions, while colder temperatures produce slower playing conditions. This is because as air gets hotter, it becomes less dense, which allows the ball to travel through it faster with less resistance. Players who are scheduling tournaments internationally should consider temperature as a factor in the events that they are looking to play.

Wind. Some places are known for being windy, for example outdoor conditions in New Zealand. Difficult wind conditions favour smart tactical players who are tough competitors prepared to adapt their game and do whatever it takes to win. Those with short tempers or who only play well when all the elements come together will generally not perform well in the wind.

Location. Most players will play their best tennis in their own country or an environment that they are comfortable in. It's quite common for Australian players to do really well on the Australia future and challenger circuit, only to go overseas and barely win a match. The closer your child plays to home, the better they will generally play, particularly if they enter tournaments with conditions that suit their game style.

Altitude. The higher the altitude, the thinner the air and the faster the playing conditions become. Most tournaments around the world are played at around sea level, but there are countries that have high-altitude events such as Sao Paulo in Brazil, Andorra in Europe or Busan in South Korea where Sam Groth recorded the world's fastest serve. Altitude can make such a big difference that the ITF only permits certain types of balls to be used in these conditions.

CASE STUDY - LUKE'S EXAMPLE

One of my coaches had a strong track record of coaching professional players and emphasised the importance of me playing in conditions that suited my unique aggressive serve-and-volley game style. I learned quickly that when I played on slower surfaces such as clay, my opponents were able to get my serve back in play more often and out-rally me from the baseline. On faster courts, I was able to get more free points on my serve and my net play became more effective. As a result, my coach set up my tournament schedule so that it focused on playing events in fast conditions to give me the edge on my opponents.

It came as no surprise that my first professional tournament win was in Pattaya in Thailand where the conditions were hot with lightning-fast conditions.

In my first year with this coach, my ATP ranking went from 900 to breaking into the world's top 450, with a big part of that being due to him picking the right tournaments to compete in and avoiding the events that didn't suit my game style.

Summary

This chapter has shown the many benefits of your child getting as much match-play experience as possible, the considerations when you're developing a match-play schedule, the different competitions for them to gain match-play experience and what to look out for in terms of match-play conditions.

Actions to consider:

- Once you are clear on your child's tennis goals, determine how many matches they need to play each year and create a yearly tournament/match-play schedule.

- Adjust the tournament/match-play schedule to ensure your child's win/loss ratio stays above 50%.

- For players with clearly developed game styles, be aware of how tournament conditions can affect performance and adapt accordingly.

SECTION 3
THE KEY DEVELOPMENT AREAS THAT PLAYERS REQUIRE

Previously I always thought it was just tactical and technique, but every match has become almost mental and physical – I try to push myself to move well. I try to push myself not to get upset and stay positive, and that's what my biggest improvement is over all those years.
— Roger Federer, *The Guardian*, 2007

7
Developing A Winning Game

> I didn't have the same fitness or ability as the other girls, so I had to beat them with my mind.
> — Martina Hingis, *The Telegraph*, 2017

The purpose of strategy on the court is to use all the tools your child has in their game to increase their chances of winning against an opponent. To do this, they need to be able to fully understand their own game, analyse their opponent, identify strengths and weaknesses, and then play an appropriate game style. Playing a large number of matches is essential to developing their tactical skills.

Understanding game styles

To maximise potential, players need to play the right game style that suits their physical and mental characteristics. Clarity on the appropriate game style will make a huge difference in the long run, so getting this wrong can be a big and costly mistake.

Different game styles

Let's start by understanding the four most common game styles.

The aggressive baseliner. This type of player enjoys being in control of the point and relies on the strength of their groundstrokes to move opponents around the court. They will go for winners aggressively from the back of the court and take calculated risks. With the forehand being the biggest groundstroke weapon in their game, baseliners typically use this to their advantage and dictate to their opponent with this shot, although some players have the ability to attack off the backhand side as well, particularly off the return of serve.

Due to their aggressive play, baseliners often find themselves with numerous opportunities to attack the net. For this reason, it pays for them to have a well-established net game. A good example of this is Rafael Nadal, who has developed his net game over the years and has had one of the highest percentages of points won on the ATP tour with over 80% success rate. Other examples of ATP/WTA professionals who are aggressive baseliners are Juan Martín del Potro and Maria Sharapova.

Counterpuncher. Being a great counterpuncher is all about wearing opponents down through consistency and having great defence. This player is usually quick around the court, has high levels of fitness, is mentally tough and plays high-percentage tennis.

When someone plays this game style effectively, unforced errors are rare. Counterpunchers usually thrive on waiting for their opponent to make a mistake. They can be tough to beat without some weapons that can finish off the point, like a big serve or forehand. The best counterpunchers keep their groundstrokes deep, and have good passing shots and lobs which make it difficult for their opponents to attack.

In 2001, Australia's Lleyton Hewitt became the world's youngest world number one by being the best counterpuncher in the game. Other examples of ATP/WTA counterpunchers are David Ferrer and Caroline Wozniacki.

Serve-and-volleyer. The serve-and-volley player will typically come into the net after the first or second serve, occasionally chip and charge from the return, and look for every opportunity in a groundstroke rally to move forward to the net. This player has an effective slice backhand which they use to approach the net as the ball can stay low, making it difficult for their opponent to hit an effective passing shot. An effective serve-and-volleyer often has a highly developed kick or topspin serve that they use to get their opponent returning from above the shoulders. This again gives more time for the player to get closer to the net, at the same time making it difficult for the opponent to hit the return low at the server's feet.

A serve-and-volleyer's typical point construction is to serve and approach the net, play a first volley either deep or into the open court, then finish the point on the second volley. When they play this game style effectively, they keep the points short and their opponent has trouble getting into any sort of rhythm throughout the match.

Changes in technology and equipment have made serve-and-volleying more difficult in recent times, but historically many of the game's greatest players have been serve-and-volleyers, such as Pete Sampras and Martina Navratilova. Examples of ATP/WTA professionals who are serve-and-volleyers are Ivo Karlović and Carla Suárez Navarro.

All-court player. The all-court player can play effectively from all parts of the court and can generally adapt his or her game to a variety of court surfaces, opponents and conditions. This player usually has all the shots, a good serve and groundstrokes, sound net play, and good use of the slice backhand and touch shots to change up the game, adapting their game and using specific tactics to exploit their opponents' weaknesses. Due to their ability to play effectively from all parts of the court, they can often have a plan A going into a match, and if it's not working, can switch to a plan B or C to get the win. Other types of player don't usually have plan B if their plan A is not working.

The only downside for an all-court player is that sometimes they have developed all parts of the game evenly and can lack a weapon or something that they are exceptionally good at. They are essentially a jack of all trades.

Examples of ATP/WTA professionals who are all-court players are Roger Federer and Agnieszka Radwańska.

How to determine what game style is right for your child

Now that you are aware of the four major game styles, you may be asking, 'What style should my child play?' You can generally find the answer to this question by looking at their physical characteristics, which indicate what game style might be more suitable. The earlier your child knows their optimum game style, the more developed their game will be in the long term.

Tall players

For male tennis players, we would categorise tall as being 190 cm and above, and for female players, 180 cm and above. These players usually have significant advantages with the serve and reach at the net.

Suitable game styles. Tall athletes who are less agile and slower around the court tend to become serve-and-volleyers, while tall players who move well are best suited to becoming all-court players.

Tactical focus. In most cases, tall players devote significant amounts of time to developing a world class serve and aggressive game style that involves getting to the net. Their main aim will be to play first-strike tennis, keep the points shorter and not give the opponents much rhythm.

Technical focus. Tall players focus on developing a near perfect service action and getting the technique spot on for this stroke. They need to schedule regular serving practice with targets a couple of times per week, and sound technical skills at the net are also essential. Their groundstroke technique should be compact and developed around power and taking the ball early.

Physical focus. Prioritise developing power characteristics over endurance, for example. Focus on staying loose, particularly through the upper body, as well as having strength in the right areas for serving and moving to the net.

Psychological focus. Tall players with big serves typically hold a high percentage of serves and break a low percentage of serves, meaning a lot of sets will be close, often coming down to the tiebreaker. They specifically need to learn how to cope with the pressure of playing big points nearly every set that they play.

Short and quick players

These players usually find it difficult to end the point due to highly developed defensive skills and foot speed. They are usually energy efficient and can wear their opponents down over the duration of a match.

Suitable game styles. Players in this category with high levels of fitness and less power tend to play the counterpuncher style, while those with stronger power characteristics tend to play more of an aggressive baseliner style.

Tactical focus. Develop high levels of consistency and topspin on the groundstrokes to improve margin for error, effective wide serves to open up the court and a weapon forehand.

Technical focus. These players need sound technique on the serve with the priority being topspin. Shorter players have to develop a heavy first and second serve as the flat serve will be low percentage due to the contact height. Groundstroke swings can be larger and facilitate more topspin and margin on the ball.

Physical focus. Speed and endurance are the biggest priorities for these players as they will win matches by slowly wearing down their opponents. High levels of fitness are a must.

Psychological focus. Short and quick players will play a lot of long matches and will need the emotional fitness to concentrate for hours at a time. They must be able to handle numerous lead swings and momentum shifts during matches due to more breaks of serve.

The power player

These players have the advantage of being able to use significant amounts of power to apply pressure and take time away from their opponents. This can be on the serve and groundstrokes.

Suitable game styles. In most cases, power players will fall into the categories of aggressive baseliner or all-court player. Being powerful, they don't have any advantage in a counterpuncher style.

Tactical focus. The power player's long-term tactical focus should be to develop all areas of their powerful game, including a sound transition and net game. The reason for this is that these types of players usually get lots of opportunities to come forward to the net to finish off the point. They can often play first-strike tennis effectively and put their opponents under pressure from the beginning of the point.

Technical focus. Having well above average racquet speed to their advantage, power players need to develop a technique that allows them to put plenty of spin on the ball as well as being able to flatten out. Spin can be a major advantage on their serve and groundstrokes.

Physical focus. Maintaining flexibility and staying injury free are crucial for this type of player. Players who hit the ball harder are placing more forces through their bodies and need to have a good pre-habilitation programme in place on top of developing all of the fundamental physical areas.

Psychological focus. Fast, powerful players need to mentally prepare themselves for longer matches and emotional fitness. Players who don't move as well will need to get really good at playing first-strike tennis and mentally prepare for shorter points.

What if your child doesn't have any standout physical qualities?

Players who have outstanding athletic qualities tend to have a strong focus on developing their physical and ball-striking abilities further, while those who may not be as powerful or are slower around the court need to look at other areas of the game to gain an advantage. Below are some suggestions that any player can turn into a weapon over the long term.

Develop a weapon serve. The serve is the most important shot in tennis, but is often the least practised. Your child's first priority is to develop with the help of an expert coach an effective service action that facilitates power, spin and accuracy. The next step is to get out on the practice court and develop a wide variety of serves combined with target practice a couple of times per week. Players with a weapon serve will have a huge advantage over their opponents, particular at college or professional level.

Become a menace at the net. Most players spend 95% of all practice and training hours on their groundstrokes, so it's not surprising to see that many junior players are poor when it comes to net play. Developing a great net game can take years, but the pay-off is worth it. In singles, it will give your child the confidence and tactical options to move forward to the net frequently and put great amounts of pressure on opponents as soon as they drop the ball short. They'll also become a huge asset in doubles as a sound net game is the key to being successful in this game.

Develop an effective slice backhand. Most physically gifted players don't give much attention to this shot, which can cause a lot of problems for opponents when it's used effectively. A player can use the slice when they're defending to provide them with time to recover. They can also use it to attack the net, lob, drop shot and generally disrupt the rhythm of the opponent. Developing an effective slice requires sound technique combined with high repetition of this shot over a number of years.

Work on mental toughness. Only a small percentage of players ever master the mental side of the game, so many are prone to large ups and downs in matches, emotional outbursts and a struggle to compete at their best when faced with adversity. This area of a player's game needs to be developed regardless of their physical characteristics as it is probably the most important aspect of the game.

Become a master at reading the play. Players who are slow with their movement can actually appear quick and always in position for the ball if they anticipate and read the play well. Your child can acquire this skill through playing a high volume of matches, picking up on opponents' habits and tendencies, understanding what parts of the court the ball is likely to hit in any given scenario in the point, and carefully observing how an opponent is setting up to hit the ball.

Become a tactician. Many great tennis athletes spend their careers developing their movement and ball striking, but often don't realise their potential in the tactical area. With enough focus on developing a versatile game style, implementing match strategy and observing opponents' tendencies, any player can become a great tactician, which can provide a big advantage over the long term.

Summary

Developing the most appropriate game style is critical for a player to maximise their potential and have the best chance of winning more often in competition. The private coach needs to play a big role in determining what game style suits the player's physique, technical ability and temperament.

Actions to consider:

- Take the time to understand the four main game styles that most players fall into.

- With help from your coach, make an assessment of your child's physical and mental qualities.

- Create a plan to make sure your child is developing the most appropriate game style to increase their chances of maximising their potential.

8
Match-Play Tactics

If Plan A isn't working, I have Plan B, Plan C, and even Plan D.
— Serena Williams, *LA Times*, 2000

When your child is developing a game plan for a match, there are a few key things they need to consider.

Analysing opponents

A lot of junior tennis players make the mistake of either not analysing their opponents in enough detail or looking at the wrong areas. As an example, a common response from a junior to the question, 'What are your opponent's strengths and weaknesses?' is 'They have a weak backhand' or 'They have a strong serve'. The issue with this type of thinking is that it lacks detail.

Follow-up questions could be:

1. What type of backhand are they weak at (wide, fast or high)?
2. What are their most effective serves (wide, T, body, flat, slice or kick, first or second serve)?
3. What about the other critical areas of their game, such as physical, mental or tactical characteristics?

At an elite level, players analyse an opponent by looking at the four key areas of the game, which are technical/ball striking, tactical, psychological and physical. Here are some examples.

Technical/ball-striking strength: a player has a great service action and huge power and accuracy on their first serve, particularly the sliding serve out wide on deuce court. Technical/ball-striking weakness: a player has a western forehand grip which causes this shot to break down when it's under pressure from power or the low ball.

Tactical strength example: a player has an all-court game and can combine a wide variety of tactics on the court with good tactical awareness. Tactical weakness: a player has a limited one-dimensional game style with no range of tactical options to consider when an opponent is outplaying them.

Psychological strength: a player fights hard for every point and loves getting into long, tough battles on the court. Psychological weakness: while they may compete hard, they are susceptible to anger and frustration when they're faced with adversity. As a result, their level can drop off dramatically.

Physical strength: a player is quick around the court and as a result defends well. Physical weakness: while a player may be fast, they lack power on all their shots including the serve, which makes them vulnerable to dropping the ball shot on groundstrokes and being pressured on their second serve.

CASE STUDY - RYAN'S STORY

I was competing in a Grade 1 16/U European Tennis Association tournament in Frankfurt, Germany, and was playing against one of the top nationally ranked German players for the age group. It was a big event with some of the best sixteen-year-olds in Europe and it was the first round.

My opponent was an amazing ball striker. He had grown up on clay and was getting the edge by overpowering me in baseline rallies, and was up a set and a break. My touring coach at the time was frustrated because if I didn't try anything different, I was going to lose the match.

One of my teammates came up to me at the change of ends, giving me a sports drink as if this was his sole intention (coaches sending messages to their players in international tournaments was common around that time, and it was almost a disadvantage if you weren't doing it, despite it not be allowed in the official rules). My teammate whispered, 'Coach says you need to slow the pace of the rally down and try to get into long, high topspin lob rallies.' At the time, I didn't know why I should do that, but I was losing anyway so I thought I would give it a go.

I did exactly what the coach had said and played high, looping topspin lobs. My opponent stayed back behind the baseline and had no choice but to return the ball in the same high, looping way. And within five or six points, the dynamic of our match had totally changed. From using his power to beat me, my opponent was now playing a slow game of patience involving thirty to forty ball rallies to decide who won the point. My opponent was still up a break of serve at this stage and every point was hard-fought. But when I got the break of serve back and we were level at four all, he became very frustrated, yelling and throwing his racquet down. As he was so impatient, he started missing shots and I won the second and third sets easily.

The lesson I learned was that if I could understand more about my opponent, then I could adapt my match strategy to play in a way that they didn't like and increase my chances of winning. In that particular tournament, I ended up winning three more matches and made the semi-finals. I would have suffered a convincing first-round loss had I not adapted my game.

CASE STUDY – LUKE'S EXAMPLE ON READING THE PLAY

I first had the opportunity to practise with Roger Federer in 2005. On the first session, we drilled for a while before playing points in a best of five tiebreaker format. My serve, which averaged over 200 km/h, was my biggest weapon and I relied on it for getting multiple free points per game against my usual opponents. Roger didn't know my game at all at that point, so I was hitting two or three aces per tiebreaker and getting a lot of free points as usual on my serve.

But after a number of practice sessions, he had learned how to read my serve and it got to the point where it was almost impossible for me to ace him. He had picked up on minor visual cues that indicated where I was going to serve, taking away my weapon and any advantage I had on my serving points. I had played many professional players on the tour on multiple occasions, but never had any of them picked up on this, which goes to show you the level of detail that the top players look for when competing.

Analysing the conditions

The conditions in which a match is played can make a huge difference to the strengths and weaknesses of each player. For example, a player with a western forehand grip will not experience too many challenges with a high-bouncing clay court as opposed to playing on a low-bouncing grass court.

The match conditions to take into consideration are:

- Court surface
- Balls
- Sun
- Wind
- Temperature
- Altitude (if applicable)

Knowing the match conditions can help your child adapt their game (or their equipment) so that they can better take advantage of their opponent's weaknesses.

Developing and implementing match strategy

Developing a match strategy is simple once you and your child know what to look for and they have practised it several times. To do this effectively, they need to accurately analyse in detail:

1. Their strengths and weaknesses (across the four key areas)
2. Their opponent's strengths and weaknesses (if they know who they are)
3. The conditions in which they will be playing the match

We have developed a template based on best-practice match thinking and encourage players to complete it before and after each match that they play. You can download this document on our website voyagertennis.com/blog

Strengths and weaknesses can be related to a specific shot (eg high, wide or fast forehand) or court speed, endurance, power, concentration, mental toughness etc. Conditions are external factors such as wind, sun, temperature, court surface, tennis balls etc, so work out how your child can use them to their advantage. If your child doesn't know their opponent, they can base their strategy on their own strengths and use the playing conditions to enhance them. If they do know their opponent, they can base their strategy on their strengths to exposure their opponent's weaknesses.

CASE STUDY - LUKE'S EXAMPLE

I qualified for the 2007 Sydney International Tournament held the week before the Australian Open. In my first round, I was drawn against a former world number one and French Open champion. It was a huge thrill to play in my home town, Sydney, against somebody I had greatly admired and respected for many years.

As I'd just spent a lot of time practising with Federer, I decided to call him up to get some advice on how to play the match. He gave me some great tips around my opponent's strengths, weaknesses and common patterns of play, where he liked to serve and where he hit his passing shots under pressure. He also said not to be intimidated as my opponent had been playing his best tennis in 1998/1999 and was now at the tail end of his career.

It was such a big help going into this match with a clear game plan. Although I didn't win it, it was one of the most memorable matches in my career because I ended up losing an 8-6 tiebreaker in the third set. The advice I'd received gave me an insight and a blueprint on what I should be looking for when planning to play against a certain opponent.

CASE STUDY - HOW NADAL BROKE A SEVEN-MATCH LOSING STREAK

For all of 2011 and the start of 2012, Novak Djokovic was dominating Rafael Nadal and had beaten him seven times in a row. One of the tactical challenges that Nadal faced, being a left hander, was that his best serves (T on the deuce court and wide on the ad court) fed right into Djokovic's major strengths (his backhand return). This meant that Nadal was struggling to consistently hold serve due to the pressure Djokovic would place him under on the first strike of each point.

In wasn't until the Monte Carlo final in April 2012 that Nadal changed his tactics and finally broke the losing streak. During this particular match, Nadal mainly stayed away from his favourite spots and hit almost every first serve to Djokovic's forehand or body throughout the entire match. This allowed Nadal to start his service points in a more positive position, and he was able to get the better of Djokovic 6/3 6/1. This was a major change from his normal patterns, which was exactly what he needed to break the seven-match losing streak.

Summary

Players need to have a deep understanding of their own game, their strengths and weaknesses as well as their opponent's, and the conditions. This will enable them to create the best possible game plan, which is crucial in mentally preparing for a match.

As a parent, you can help evaluate your child's performance in a structured manner to reinforce strengths, embed learnings and remove some of the negative emotions that might remain after the game.

Actions to consider:

- Provide opportunities for your child to develop their analytical skills around their opponents and the match conditions.

- Download the match preparation worksheet so that your child can complete it before and after each competitive match at voyagertennis.com, FAQS & Resources, Blog and downloads.

9
Good Technique And The Right Equipment

> I made it look so easy on court all those years. No one realized how hard I had to work.
> — Pete Sampras, *ATP Insider*, 2002

The purpose of a player having good technique is for them to be able to execute a wide variety of tactics against an opponent and play all shots with consistency and confidence. If players have technical flaws, they will have holes in their game that their opponents will be able to exploit. It is important to establish good technical foundations at a young age (primary school ideally), which is relatively easy to do with the right coach and training programme.

For elite players, a long-term private coach/mentor is important. Their initial focus is to develop technical foundations, then address any bad habits that may creep in. At the end of the day, technique doesn't have to be perfect; just 85–90% of optimal is enough in most cases.

As an example, Rafael Nadal won at least six grand slams early in his career with a suboptimal service action, which he addressed prior to winning his first US Open in 2010. Novak Djokovic had a glitch in his forehand backswing early in his career when he was among the top ten in the world. These issues didn't stop either player from becoming great, and they both addressed the issues at the right time for them.

A coach for an elite player takes on the role of mentor, helping the player identify and take ownership of areas that he or she needs to address, take action and grow as a result. The technical side is only one aspect of this, although this is not to say a focus on the technical side with private coaching isn't warranted early in a child's tennis development.

Below is a checklist that coaches can use to assess the level of a player's technical competence. The checklist is broad in nature and assumes coaches who work with elite players understand all of the fundamental grips, swings and footwork patterns.

TECHNICAL FUNDAMENTALS CHECKLIST

Player name:_____ Date:_____

GENERAL
- [ ] Always commits to great positioning and contacting the ball between hip and shoulder height
- [ ] Uses 100% racquet speed when appropriate
- [ ] Hits every groundstroke within reason with adequate levels of topspin

STROKE ANALYSIS

Forehand
- [ ] Uses a fundamental grip
- [ ] Fluent circular swing
- [ ] Appropriate footwork

Backhand
- [ ] Uses a fundamental grip
- [ ] Fluent circular swing
- [ ] Appropriate footwork

Slice backhand
- [ ] Continental grip
- [ ] High to low swing
- [ ] Appropriate footwork

Overhead
- [ ] Continental grip
- [ ] Early preparation of throwing position
- [ ] Appropriate footwork

Forehand volley
- [ ] Continental grip
- [ ] Compact swing
- [ ] Appropriate footwork
- [ ] Maintains a low centre of gravity

Backhand volley
- [ ] Continental grip
- [ ] Compact swing
- [ ] Appropriate footwork
- [ ] Maintains a low centre of gravity

Serve
- [ ] Continental grip
- [ ] Appropriate feet position
- [ ] Suitable ball toss
- [ ] Effective use of legs
- [ ] 90 degree throwing position
- [ ] Contact point facilitates variety of spins

Figure 9.1 Technical fundamentals checklist

The role of the private coach

> However great your dedication, you never win anything on your own.
> — Rafael Nadal, *Rafa*, 2011

Many parents without a professional tennis background struggle with understanding all the requirements to help their child become a successful player, so it's important to have a support structure in place to guide you through these areas. An effective high-performance coach can play a huge role in helping you put the critical elements together. The private coach will develop a player's technical fundamentals at an early age, constantly prioritising the most important areas for the player to work on over each stage of their development.

Beside the technical component, parents often rely on a mentor who has the skills and experience to guide them and their child through the many other facets of the game, including tournament scheduling and match-play recommendations, structuring an on-court and physical training plan, goal setting and measuring progress, developing an appropriate game style for the player that aligns with their physical and mental characteristics, reading the play and opponents' strengths and weaknesses, and establishing in-between-point routines. Other areas of guidance may include:

- Warm-up and cool-down routines
- Understanding and implementing patterns of play
- Creating match plans and strategies for competition
- Tips on how to stay mentally tough when faced with adversity in matches

- Encouraging the development of a strong work ethic and character
- Balancing tennis and education
- Pathways available through private school scholarships, club tennis, US college scholarships, European Club Tennis, etc

The private coach should also have the ability to outsource and refer players to specialists for:

- Physical development
- Psychological development
- Nutrition
- US college guidance and placement (for high school students in Year 9 and above)

How to choose a private coach

In almost every major city, there is an abundance of tennis coaches available to new clients. The biggest challenge is finding one who is suitable and effective at working with elite players.

These are the things to consider when you're choosing a high-performance coach with regard to their skills and experience:

- Are they qualified?

- Have they undergone all the relevant checks for working with children?

- Do they specialise in working with elite tennis players?

- Do they have a strong background as a player, ideally a former nationally ranked junior who reached a US college or European club tennis standard or higher? There are always exceptions to the rule, but in the majority of cases, it's usually better to work with somebody who's been there before.

The coach you choose will be an important role model for your child and you may also want to ask yourself some of the following questions to explore the coaches' personal qualities and teaching style:

- Are they reliable?

- Do they have good communication skills and are they easy to build a rapport with?

- Do they have the best interests of the student at heart?

- Do they customise training to suit the student's individual learning style?

- Do they regularly provide high-quality and specific feedback?

GOOD TECHNIQUE AND THE RIGHT EQUIPMENT

- Do they work on a couple of components per lesson and focus on the fundamentals the majority of the time?

- Do they understand that the parents are on the journey as much as the students are and provide guidance to parents as well?

Common mistakes that parents make with private lessons

Having multiple private coaches. In almost all cases, a quality high-performance coach will provide everything that a player needs and will have a specific plan for their development. Having two or more coaches is likely to lead to mixed messages and confuse the player, which will halt their progress. One coach is a lot more cost-efficient and delivers far better long-term results than multiple coaches.

Valuing private lessons over training and competition. Private coaching for an elite player ideally makes up a small percentage of total court time. The rest should be dedicated to training and match play. Keep private coaching in perspective. The more technically sound a player gets, the less time they will need to dedicate to private lessons.

Getting too many lessons. Each private lesson should focus a player on one to three things to go away and work on in their training or match play. It is then the player's responsibility to practise those key areas before seeing the coach again, so players need enough time between lessons to do this.

We often find that players who get lessons too frequently (multiple times in a week) take less responsibility for their game and become reliant on their coach telling them what to do. Great players take ownership of their game and need time to work things out themselves. Regular weekly or, in some cases, fortnightly lessons are optimal for junior players to effectively develop their game.

Being inconsistent. Consistency is an important aspect of progress. If you've booked a regular lesson for your child with a coach, make sure that you maintain your commitment. Repeatedly cancelling your child's lessons will likely slow their progress and increase the chances of your coach giving your child's time slot to another player who will be there every week.

On the flip side, if your coach is cancelling too often, then put them on notice or get a new coach.

CASE STUDY – RYAN'S EXAMPLE

I started out with a fifteen-minute lesson each week as a seven-year-old and was given one thing to practise. This slowly progressed up to one hour a week by the age of ten, then from age fourteen I moved overseas, then to the AIS.

I didn't have many private lessons over that period. Once my technique was reasonably sound, all the gains came from playing competitive matches, on court and physical training. What I did have was some incredible coaches in the AIS. They were strong mentors who kept a close eye on my game and made sure I was working on the most appropriate areas of it every day.

CASE STUDY – LUKE'S EXAMPLE

I was really fortunate to be coached by Kim Warwick who was a former Australian number one, grand-slam singles finalist and six-time grand-slam doubles champion. On the first session, he got me straight into point play to assess my game. He noted that I was a pretty good athlete, had a good serve, decent forehand, was OK around the net, but my slice backhand needed work as this was critical to my all-court game style. He gave me some technical coaching on how to effectively hit a slice backhand, then he told me to go away and practise it, which I did.

A week later at the next lesson, Kim fed the first ball to my slice backhand. As soon as I hit it, he caught the ball and asked me to come up to the net for a chat.

'How long have you been practising this shot since the last lesson?' he asked.

'About ten hours against the wall and against my older brother, Bart,' I replied.

He was impressed with my dedication, and after I'd hit another ten to fifteen more slice backhands, he said, 'You've got this shot to where you need it for now. Keep working on it and let's move on to the next area of development of your game.'

One reason I had such rapid progress under Kim's guidance what that he'd give me something to work on and I'd go away and practise it like crazy, and often by the time I saw him next, we would be able to move on to the next area of development. This allowed me to progress the technical aspect of my game four to five times faster than other players who relied on their lesson time to practise their technique.

Achieving the optimal balance

To bring out a tennis player's full potential, private coaching is one of the three parts of on-court development.

Competition. Match play will provide the ultimate feedback about how your child's game is progressing. If they didn't win the match, it is because their opponent did one or a number of things better than they did on the day. It's important to acknowledge these areas and work on them.

Private lessons. This is where your child spends time one-on-one with their coach to improve the areas of their game that need the most amount of attention.

Squads. These are group training sessions with peers of a similar level where your child can work on the areas that their private coach has decided need practice and develop tactical skills, fitness, and generally get a lot of repetition of shots with intensity and purpose.

A successful development cycle works something like this:

- Your child competes in a tournament/s and receives feedback on how their game is performing under competitive match-play conditions
- They work with their private coach on the areas that need improving to help them perform better in competition
- They get lots of practice in squads to develop the specific areas that they and their private coach are working on
- They keep repeating cycle

Choosing the optimal equipment

A lot of tennis players don't realise how big an impact the equipment they use can have on their performance. In this section, we will briefly explain some things to consider around the racquets, strings and footwear to use when your child is training or competing.

Racquets

Junior tennis players will often choose the racquet used by their favourite player by default, but this particular type of racquet may not be suitable for their physical characteristics or game style. Each racquet has five key areas to consider which influence its output.

1. Head size. Power is directly related to the head size of the racquet, and generally the larger the head size, the more powerful the racquet will be. A larger head also offers a larger hitting area and sweet spot, which results in more forgiveness when a player doesn't connect the ball with the centre of the strings at contact.

Today's racquets are offered in head sizes ranging from 93 to 135 square inches, with elite junior players generally looking to use racquets in the 96–100 square inches range. Racquets around 100 square inches tend to offer a good balance of power and control for most players.

2. Length. The standard length for an adult tennis racquet is 27 inches, but racquets are available in lengths ranging from 19 to 29 inches (29 inches is the legal maximum for tournament play). A longer racquet provides more reach and slightly more power overall than standard-length racquets, although the added length results in a higher swing weight, which means a little more effort to manoeuvre the racquet. Most

GOOD TECHNIQUE AND THE RIGHT EQUIPMENT

professional players use a racquet that is 27 or 27.5 inches in length.

Elite players need to seek the advice of an experienced tennis professional with regards to racquet length as using full-size racquets at an early age can be detrimental and cause injury.

3. Weight. For junior players, lighter racquets are more manoeuvrable and allow the player to develop good technical fundamentals by controlling the racquet more easily and hitting with more topspin. Heavier racquets can provide more power as a player matures physically and becomes ready for it, but the main mistake we see juniors make is increasing the weight of the racquet too early, which increases the chances of developing poor technique and injuries.

A standard weight of a full-size racquet is around 300 g, and in today's game most top-level pros have racquets between 330 g and 340 g. Players should only consider getting a 300 g racquet some time in the teenage years or when they are physically ready for it. Once again, consult an experienced tennis professional when you are looking to increase the weight of your child's racquet. Keep in mind that you can always add weight to a racquet if it's too light, but reducing racquet weight is almost impossible.

4. String pattern. This can often be overlooked by players. String patterns are open (fewer strings and more open space) or closed (more strings and less open space). Open string patterns typically produce more power and spin on the ball, but slightly reduce string durability. Some common open string patterns are sixteen by sixteen (sixteen main strings and sixteen cross strings) and sixteen by fifteen. They will deflect more on impact than a denser pattern, providing greater ball rebound and feeling livelier.

Closed string patterns (such as eighteen by twenty) will generally provide less power but more ball control and durability. Neutral string patterns that are in between, such as sixteen by nineteen and sixteen by eighteen, provide the best of both worlds by having a combination of power and control.

Before considering the string pattern of a racquet, players need to have a clear idea of what characteristics they are looking for, eg more power or control.

5. Grip sizes. Having the right grip size will help your child perform on the court. Using the wrong size can lead to poor performance and even injuries to the hand, wrist or elbow. Generally, the smaller the grip, the more a player will be able to manoeuvre the racquet and produce spin, while large grip sizes are less manoeuvrable and as a result generally produce a flatter outcome on each shot.

GOOD TECHNIQUE AND THE RIGHT EQUIPMENT

Below are some of the common grip sizes:

- 4⅛ inches / grip size 1 (smallest)
- 4¼ inches / grip size 2
- 4⅜ inches / grip size 3
- 4½ inches / grip size 4 (largest)

Reportedly, Roger Federer uses a 4⅜ inch grip size 3, while Rafael Nadal uses a 4¼ inch grip size 2. Both play with overwraps, which builds the grip up to a degree.

When you're selecting a racquet and testing a grip size for your child, encourage them to take a few air swings – if it feels comfortable and their fingers and palm are not touching but are not too far apart either, then you've probably found the right size grip.

Strings

For most players, strings are just an afterthought. They spend a lot of time researching racquets, but only a few seconds choosing strings, but not all strings (and string tensions) are correct for every player. Everyone has different needs and preferences.

Here are some of the key components to consider when you're choosing strings.

What are they made of? There are now hundreds of strings available on the market so we'll summarise the most common types.

Natural gut is the Rolls Royce of tennis string, providing top-of-the-line tension maintenance and feel for players of all ability levels. This is a common string among professional players due to the power and feel it provides. The downside of natural gut is that it is generally the most expensive type of string and doesn't last as long as the others.

Polyester strings are generally stiff and durable and are great for producing spin on the ball. They are popular on the pro tour for this reason with many pros combining a stiffer string (polyester) with a softer string like natural gut to achieve maximum power, spin and feel on the ball. As an example, Roger Federer uses natural gut for his main strings, and Luxilon ALU Power Rough (part polyester) for his cross strings. Some common polyester strings are Babolat RPM blast, Luxilon Big Banger Ace and Babolat Pro Hurricane Tour.

Synthetic gut is the most economical of the various string families. It is a nylon-based string which attempts to provide similar characteristics to natural gut with power and feel, although in most cases it is not quite as good. Elite players who use synthetic gut will often combine it with a polyester string to enhance spin and durability qualities.

GOOD TECHNIQUE AND THE RIGHT EQUIPMENT

Multifilament is a type of string design where numerous individual filaments are combined together into a single length. These strings tend to produce more power and comfort than synthetic gut strings and are a preferred choice for players with arm problems. Designed to mimic the performance of natural gut without the price tag, these strings provide excellent elasticity when freshly strung, but lose tension quicker than natural gut.

There is always a compromise between playability and durability, with natural gut and multifilament strings being the most playable and polyester strings being the most durable. Players need to thoroughly test different types of string to help them decide which will suit their playing style.

Gauge/thickness. This is the diameter of the string, commonly expressed in millimetres and/or gauge numbers. The most common string thickness for elite players is between 1.20 mm and 1.30 mm. Thinner strings tend to provide more power, feel and spin potential than a larger diameter string of the same type, although the thicker string will provide more control and durability.

String tension. Every racquet has a recommended tension that the manufacturer provides. We recommend you choose a tension within this range.

Generally speaking, the tighter the tension, the more control players will get with less power. This is recommended for more advanced players who can generate a lot of power themselves and need greater precision. Conversely, looser strings will provide more power with less control.

Most professional players have racquets strung between 45–65 pounds with everybody having their own personal preference. As an example, professional doubles players Mike and Bob Bryan tend to get their racquets strung around 45 pounds, while the Williams sisters are up around 65 pounds of tension.

It's quite common for professional players to adjust their string tension in different playing conditions. For example, in fast conditions they'll often increase their string tension (to gain control), while in slower conditions they'll lower the string tension (to increase power).

Tennis shoes

It goes without saying that elite tennis players need to wear shoes that are specifically designed for tennis. With all the stop/start and lateral movements required, players need to ensure that their shoes provide ankle support, cushioning and the traction to change direction quickly. Using the wrong shoes can cause injury and poor performance, so this section

GOOD TECHNIQUE AND THE RIGHT EQUIPMENT

will explain the most common types of tennis shoes to consider, depending on what surface your child is playing on.

Hardcourt. Shoes for hardcourts need to have good cushioning and bounce back from an unforgiving surface. These shoes also need tough outer soles so they don't wear out too quickly.

Clay court. Usually, shoes for clay court have a softer zigzag pattern underneath which provides grip when players are sliding on slippery surfaces. These shoes can also be used on sandy synthetic grass or natural grass courts to prevent excessive sliding.

Grass court. Finding shoes for the grass court can be quite difficult. They have soft dimples under the shoe to help with change of direction and grip on the court, and can also be used on synthetic grass.

The most common mistake we see players make is using the wrong shoe for the playing surface, which can significantly hinder performance. For example, if a player is wearing a hardcourt shoe to play on a slippery surface like clay or synthetic grass, their movement will suffer and their performance will be much lower than they'd expect. Wearing old shoes without much tread underneath is another common mistake with similar consequences.

Summary

A good, solid, repeatable and reliable technique is important to develop your child at a young age and a private coach can be invaluable during this period. As your child's tennis skills develop, the private coach becomes less important from a technique perspective, but a mentor to guide them through the elite-player journey becomes more important. Also, ensure your child is using appropriate tennis equipment to help maximise their technical skills and reduce the chances of injury.

Actions to consider:

- Ensure your child develops good technical fundamentals at a young age (primary/early high school).

- Seek a private coach/mentor for you and your child who can guide you through all of the aspects of the elite-player journey.

- Seek the advice of an experienced tennis professional to ensure your child is using the most appropriate tennis equipment.

10
Developing A High-Performance Athlete

> There is no way around the hard work. Embrace it.
> — Roger Federer, 2013

> Tennis takes care of everything... In addition to toning your arms and shoulders, it's a total body workout for your legs and abs, and works your heart and core unlike any other sport.
> — Samantha Stosur, *Self*, 2012

Physical development is vital for a player to be able to perform at their best day in, day out, week in, week out, every year for potentially twenty years or more. It is also hugely important for junior players so that they can stay healthy and accomplish the training volume they require to be world class. Tennis players are becoming more and more powerful and fit, so they need physical development for the strength, speed, agility, flexibility and stamina to compete.

Tennis is a repetitive sport with players using the same motions/actions up to thousands of times each week. This can place a lot of stress on specific parts of the body. Preventing injuries, whether repetitive or impact, is crucial as they are the number one cause of setbacks to a player's improvement. Yet despite the fact that injuries can have the most serious consequences, they are perhaps the most neglected area of a player's development.

A lot of the time, players can prevent injuries if they identify problem areas early and put a programme in place. An appropriate pre- and post-training and match-play routine is key in preventing injuries, as well as players priming themselves mentally. Many of the greats of the game prioritise physical conditioning and longevity above all else and invest significant resources in expert physical trainers.

Injury prevention

Injuries among young tennis players have two big downsides. Firstly, they obviously prevent players from training and playing matches, and the second downside, which is often overlooked, is that recovering from injury and doing the necessary rehabilitation is time consuming, repetitive and boring. It is a time when players can lose their passion for the game and get distracted by other things in their lives, so we highly recommend a structured approach to injury prevention.

Different body types, game styles and techniques are prone to different types of injury. To determine the most effective injury-prevention approach, we suggest that every elite tennis player who plans on playing the game for more than a couple of years has a detailed physical screening/assessment. This will analyse all the joints and muscles in the player's body, their strengths, weaknesses, areas of flexibility and inflexibility, and identify any areas of the body that will be susceptible to injury in the future.

A physical screening will typically provide a player with a detailed report on each area of the body that it has tested and analysed, as well as recommendations on what to work on to prevent injuries in the future. It's vitally important players follow recommendations as their bodies need to stay largely injury free for a decade or two.

Physical screenings are usually available in most cities and delivered by physios specialising in elite sports.

CASE STUDY – RYAN'S EXPERIENCE AT THE AIS

One of the first things I underwent at the AIS was a detailed physical assessment. Every player got a report with 'red flags' for areas of the body that were at high risk of being injured in the future if they weren't worked on in a physical programme. A standard report for most players showed one or two red-flag areas, but when I received my report, there were red flags in almost all areas of my body. It was by far the worst physical report of all the tennis players in my group.

Although I'd had a relatively injury-free playing career up to that point, the report was showing me that if I didn't take significant immediate action, then the stresses that I would be placing on my body over the period ahead would be too much and it would break down with injury. This was real wake-up call for me and I worked incredibly hard every day to reduce the chances of injury in all the areas identified in my report.

This appeared to work really well, and I got through two more years of being injury free before the repetitive injuries started occurring one after the other. In my eighteenth birth year (last year of juniors) I played for nine months of the year with three months out because of repetitive injuries. In my nineteenth birth year, I played for six months with six months of injury time out, and in my twentieth year, I made an easy decision to call it a day and begin my career as a professional tennis coach.

Upon reflecting on this, I realised that I would have benefitted from a screening at a younger age which could have allowed me to prevent a lot of the injuries that occurred. At the age of fifteen, I'd likely left it too late to find out.

To this day, I love being physically active with coaching and enjoy regularly engaging in recreational sports, but it is vital for players and parents to understand the high physical demands that are placed on the body when players are competing on the professional tour and the importance of preparing the body for it.

Joint and muscle mobility

In today's game, the top tennis players have a great range of motion and flexibility, Novak Djokovic and Grigor Dimitrov being perhaps the two best examples of this on the tour. Flexible muscles and joints enhance movement and power and reduce the chances of repetitive injury. When a joint or muscle lacks flexibility, it will often not be able to function effectively. The body will then compensate by using other areas to do the work instead. A lot of repetitive injuries are caused by a lack of mobility and can be prevented if treated early enough.

A daily flexibility routine is essential for all players to maintain and improve their range of motion. Activities like yoga can provide great benefits in this area.

CASE STUDY – THE BENEFIT OF A ROUTINE (LUKE BOURGEOIS)

I understood the importance of maintaining flexibility at a young age. My coaches drilled into my head that good flexibility would result in more power, faster movement and injury prevention.

From high school onwards, I got into the habit of a daily flexibility routine for stretching my arms, back, groin, glutes, calves and other muscle groups. I developed some quality warm-up routines that involved elevating my heart rate, dynamic stretching and anything that would prepare my body for the intense physical demands of practice or match play. I also made sure I cooled down correctly to assist in speeding up recovery times.

I have no doubt these habits extended my tennis career and allowed me to play competitive tennis for thirty years with few injuries or niggles.

Speed/agility

It all starts with the footwork.
— Roger Federer, *Tennis.com*, 2014

Elite tennis is being played at an increasingly fast pace, so speed and agility are key for all game styles. The purpose of being fast and agile is to enhance a player's ability not just to get to balls, but to effectively position their bodies for every shot they play.

Players who are always in position can play with power, rarely make unforced errors, are difficult to hit winners against and are generally tough to beat.

The following three factors play the biggest role in a player consistently being able to set up effectively for each shot.

Anticipation and reading the play

Players often have less than a second from the time their opponent strikes the ball to the time they have to be returning it. The ability to anticipate and read the play is a skill they acquire through a high volume of training hours and match play along with watching opponents, learning carefully when they strike the ball and observing common patterns.

Tennis-specific footwork patterns

All elite players need to develop tennis footwork patterns for moving to the ball, setting up for the ball, recovering and reacting. Most high-performance coaches will teach these patterns so that a player can move effectively on the court.

Movement from A to B

The average number of steps it takes to get to the ball in tennis is four and it's important to keep this in mind when you're creating a speed/agility training plan with your child. Some players make the mistake of doing endless 100–200 metre sprints when in reality this type of movement is not required on the court.

Roger Federer's long-term physical trainer Pierre Paganini advises, 'You have to be strong, fast, coordinated and have endurance in tennis … But you also should never forget you have to use this on a tennis court… the speed is in the first three steps and then you're playing the tennis ball. So you have to train to be particularly strong in the first three steps.'[17]

Players who are training to improve their speed/agility do so by creating speed exercises over short distances with lots of changes of direction to mimic the realities of the tennis court.

Another point to keep in mind is that speed/agility is largely influenced by the player's range of motion/flexibility and strength.

Strength

Strength training for athletes is critical for the development of speed and power on the tennis court. Ideally tennis players will stay light and flexible while

---

[17] Christopher Clarey, 'The Secret to Roger Federer's Success is This Man', *The New York Times* (2017) www.nytimes.com/2017/11/12/sports/tennis/roger-federer-atp-finals.html

improving their strength, core stability and power qualities. We would strongly recommend you look for a tennis-specific trainer for your child as there are two common mistakes players can make when it comes to strength work.

Putting on too much muscle

Having muscle mass (particularly through the upper body) may look good when a player is at the beach, but it certainly won't do them any favours when it comes to performing on the tennis court. Players who get too bulky often end up with knee troubles.

Losing flexibility

As muscles get bulkier, they can cause flexibility issues. Players don't want to gain strength at the expense of flexibility as this will reduce the power they can produce and increase their chances of injury in the long run.

CASE STUDY - RYAN'S EXPERIENCE

One of the mistakes some tennis players make is to do weight training that causes bulky muscles, particularly in the upper body. I made this mistake myself and suffered from being slower around the court and having knee injuries due to the extra weight I was carrying.

After spending some time in the grand-slam locker rooms, I was surprised to see how thin the best players in the world were. Most were toned, but had no bulk whatsoever in the upper body, which allowed them to be much quicker around the court. In most cases, a player produces the majority of their power when they have a body that functions optimally in all areas, a good range of motion (flexibility) and sound technique.

Endurance

The best players in the world repeatedly play points with high intensity for hours at a time without any drops in their high-quality play. This can only come with high levels of endurance.

Players with low levels of endurance usually suffer from the following in matches:

- Playing with low intensity. They subconsciously know they can't sustain a high intensity over three or five sets and are forced to coast or pace themselves over a full match.

- Making unforced errors due to poor decisions in relation to trying to finish the point off too early.

- More displays of anger and emotional outbursts. Particularly in demanding matches, the unfit player may feel a lot of physical pain relating to pushing themselves to stay in the match.

When a player feels physical pain, they are more susceptible to emotional outbursts and losing their temper.

The nature of a tennis match is that a player will have a work to rest ratio somewhere between one to one and one to five. As an example, a long point that lasts fifteen seconds with a fifteen-second break in between points would equate to a one to one work to rest ratio, while a short point lasting three seconds with a fifteen-second break would equate to a one to five work to rest ratio. Point duration in a competitive tennis match will typically range from three to fifteen seconds in length and will usually be played over 100–200 points in total, so players need to train their bodies to handle this type of intense activity.

You may be asking yourself, 'What is the best way to increase match play endurance?' The answer is obvious and simple:

Play more matches.

Playing a high volume of tough, competitive matches is one of the best ways to increase tennis-specific endurance. Most professional players that you see on television today have played thousands of matches and their bodies are so accustomed to the rhythm of a match that they are able to play their best over three sets without fatigue affecting their performance at all.

Players can develop endurance on a bike, going for long runs and, more specifically, via speed endurance training sessions where they train at high intensity with multiple periods of rest recovery throughout the session.

Managing growth spurts

Every person experiences growth spurts at different times, which can have a big impact, particularly on an individual's speed and power. Players who experience a major growth spurt earlier than their peer group will often have an advantage for a while until the others catch up. It is important that parents and players watch out for growth-related injuries when the players are going through these spurts.

CASE STUDY – LUKE'S EXAMPLE

I was one of the players who experienced a late growth spurt, and at the age of fourteen I was small compared to my peer group. I was ranked around number fifty-five in the state for my age group, and when I shook hands with my opponents, they were often nearly a foot taller than me.

My idols growing up were Stefan Edberg and Pat Cash, and I have many vivid memories of watching them play, particularly Cash winning Wimbledon in 1987. As a young kid, I would watch them coming to the net and finishing the point time and time again, and I copied that into the way I played the game. From age ten onwards, I would take any opportunity to move forward to the net and try to finish the point. The big issue that I had was that I wasn't big enough to cover the net properly, which resulted in me losing a lot more than I would have had I stayed back on the baseline and tried to out-rally my opponents.

This all changed when I was fifteen and had a large growth spurt, adding 30 cm to my height. I grew into my attacking game style all of a sudden as I was more powerful, and I jumped from ranking fifty-five in the state for my age group to making the finals in the nationals and becoming number one in the country within eighteen months. At the age of seventeen, I won a junior grand slam in doubles.

Summary

Physical development is vital for a player to perform at their best. It is also hugely important for junior players so that they can stay healthy and injury free to complete the training and match-play volume they require to become world class. Physical development is essential for players to gain the necessary strength, speed, agility, flexibility and stamina to compete at a high level.

Actions to consider:

- Book your child in for a physical screening to identify any potential injuries they could be at risk from in the future. Providers such as Precision Athletica in Sydney deliver a professional physical screening along with other areas of athletic development.

- Ensure your child has a regular pre-habilitation programme in place that they consistently follow.

- After you've got the pre-habilitation programme in place successfully, look for a trainer who can help design a tennis-specific physical programme to enhance your child's other physical qualities.

- Develop a pre-match and pre-training warm-up routine that your child uses day in, day out so it becomes habitual.

11
Fuelling A High-Performance Athlete

> Exercise is king. Nutrition is queen.
> — Jack LaLanne, fitness, exercise and nutrition expert, *Finding Your Own Fountain of Youth*, 2008

The quality of the fuel – the food and drink – that a tennis player consumes has a direct impact on his or her performance. People generally are becoming increasingly aware of the need to eat healthily, but often we see tennis players struggle to make good nutrition choices, which may come as no surprise given the amount of poor food choices readily available and discipline required to avoid them. It can be difficult for players to link their nutrition directly to its impact on their physical readiness to train and play, but in our experience, poor nutrition choices lead to lower energy, bad moods, players getting sick more often and longer recovery times during a training or competition period.

It takes time, knowledge and discipline to develop good nutrition habits, but eating and drinking healthily is well worth the effort. It can have these direct benefits for tennis:

- Sustained energy, which allows players to train harder for longer and improve at a faster rate

- Performance in competition improves as players can compete at a high level over long periods of time

- Recovery time is faster after long training sessions and matches, and players can back up performances the next day more easily

It also has other benefits over and above sporting performance:

- Better energy and increased alertness

- Stronger immune system, so the person gets sick less often

- An increase in the chances of them having good mental health

Mental health issues among children are on the rise in Australia and other countries, but research has shown that good nutrition and mental health have strong links to each other.[18]

CASE STUDY – THE IMPORTANCE OF NUTRITION

Prior to 2011, Novak Djokovic had cemented himself as a top-five player and had won one grand slam in 2008, although he was suffering regular mid-match collapses which were causing physical symptoms such as difficulty breathing, dizziness, lethargy and occasionally vomiting.

A family friend and nutritionist, Igor Četojević, witnessed Djokovic's mid-match physical breakdowns on several occasions and suggested he get his blood tested for allergies and intolerances, which he did around the middle of 2010. The blood test result showed that Djokovic was strongly intolerant to wheat and dairy products, which were in foods that he was regularly consuming. Being told to stop eating bread, pasta and cheese was not the best news for Djokovic as he loved these foods and his parents even owned a pizza restaurant, but given the physical challenges he was experiencing, he was willing to give it a go.

Četojević asked Djokovic to try a new gluten-free diet for two weeks and the results were immediate. Djokovic felt lighter, he had more energy and was sleeping better. When it was suggested a week later that he eat a bagel, the negative impact was instant. Djokovic felt sluggish and dizzy.

---

[18] E. Selhub, 'Nutritional psychiatry: Your brain on food' (2018) www.health.harvard.edu/blog/nutritional-psychiatry-your-brain-on-food-201511168626

When he switched to a gluten-free diet, the benefits were decisive. Immediately after the diet change, in December 2010, Djokovic started one of the longest winning streaks in the history of the game, winning forty-three matches in a row including the Australian Open. He became world number one for the first time in July 2011.

With the new diet, he shed 4 kg in weight and felt stronger, mentally sharper and healthier than ever before. Since the change of diet and to date, Djokovic has won an additional thirteen grand slams.[19]

The Djokovic example shows the importance of nutrition and how it relates to performance on the court. The following section includes information about the main food groups and how players can use them to their advantage.

The food groups

Carbohydrates

Carbohydrates are the body's main source of energy. It is important to understand the Glycaemic Index (GI) of different carbohydrates as this can have a significant impact on athletic performance and general energy levels. Low GI options provide a *long-lasting source of energy*. These foods cause a steady rise in the

---

[19] P. Newman, 'Revealed: The diet that saved Novak Djokovic' (2013) www.frasercoastchronicle.com.au/news/revealed-diet-saved-novak-djokovic/1992684

level of glucose in the blood, which in turn leads to a small and gentle rise in insulin and a more sustained release of energy.

Example of low GI foods include legumes, rolled oats (porridge), brown rice, red/black quinoa, corn, sweet potato, most fruit, wholegrain sourdough bread. Some examples of whole carbs (unprocessed foods that contain the fibre found naturally in the food) include vegetables, whole fruit, potatoes and whole-grains.

High GI carbohydrates create a large surge in insulin and will start reactions in the body that leave you feeling lethargic, hungry and craving more sugar, so avoid these. Examples of high GI foods include instant oats, low-fibre cereals, white and wholemeal bread, pasta, canned spaghetti, sushi rice, medium-grain white rice, jasmine rice, couscous, French fries, and potato (most white varieties).

For a comprehensive GI index list of foods visit www.the-gi-diet.org/lowgifoods/

Protein

Protein is important for growth and development, as well as the recovery of muscles, so choosing good-quality sources of protein is essential. The best way to aid muscle recovery is by including protein with every meal across the day and choosing a variety of different protein sources across the week.

Examples of foods that are good sources of protein include seafood, white-meat poultry, eggs, beans, soy, lean beef and tofu. Red meat is a good protein source as well, although it can take between twenty-four and seventy-two hours to digest, which may not be ideal for athletes looking to perform day in, day out.

Fats

Healthy fats are an important component of a diet as they provide energy, vitamins and essential fatty acids, and generally make us feel fuller for longer. Fats are high in energy (or calories/kJ) and take a long time to digest, so only eat them in small portion sizes.

Some examples of good fats are olive oil, avocado, nuts and seeds, and fatty fish like salmon. Some examples of bad fats are fatty cuts of beef, pork, and lamb, high-fat dairy foods such as whole milk, butter, cheese, sour cream, ice cream, and tropical oils such as coconut oil, palm oil, cocoa butter.

Fruit and vegetables

Fruit and vegetables provide the body with essential nutrients such as fibre, vitamins and minerals that all help to aid performance and recovery, and each different coloured vegetable provides different nutrients, so make sure to eat different coloured vegetables every day. Vegetables are lower in energy than other foods, so they can be included in the diet in large quantities. Every athlete should aim to get at least five servings of fruit and vegetables per day.

Hydration

Hydration is absolutely essential on match and training days. If your child is dehydrated, they will not only struggle to perform, they could end up feeling really sick by the end of the day. These are some of the symptoms, which have a negative impact on performance, that they can experience by being dehydrated:

- Early fatigue
- Nausea
- Vomiting
- Muscle cramping
- Dizziness

To prevent this, athletes who are in training or competition phase hydrate the day before with plenty of water. A good measurement of hydration is the colour of the urine. Clear to pale yellow is hydrated, and the darker it is, the more dehydrated the person is.

Another thing a player can do between matches and training is to have a drink with added electrolytes. This is particularly good on hot days when players lose a lot of fluid from sweating. Sports drinks provide electrolytes and glucose (carbohydrates/sugar), which help the body to hold on to water and stay hydrated while providing more energy. It's important to know that sports drinks such as Gatorade and Powerade are high in sugar so only use them when your child really needs them on match days. Water is the best choice of drink on a regular day-to-day basis.

Main meals guide

For main meals such as lunch and dinner, aim to achieve the right balance of carbs and proteins for athletes:

- 50% vegetables, at least two types
- 25% wholegrains/low GI carbohydrates
- 25% protein

At breakfast time, it may not be realistic to have half a plate of veg, so this is a good time for your child to get their fruit intake.

Foods to avoid

These foods may taste good, but will be counterproductive to an athlete's performance:

- Snacks high in sugar, such as cakes, biscuits, chocolate, lollies, ice cream
- Drinks high in sugar, such as fruit juices and soft drinks
- Fast foods such as chips and pizza
- Deep fried foods
- Takeaways
- Pastries
- Processed meat

These foods are not designed for athletes and can make a person feel sluggish and lethargic. They may also result in weight gain, which can slow a player down and reduce endurance levels.

If your child has bad habits in the area of nutrition and is looking to make changes, please be patient. It can take six to twelve months to adopt new eating behaviours before they become automatic, but the rewards are well worth it.

Summary

The quality of the fuel that a tennis player consumes has a direct impact on the quality of his or her performance during the course of a match, tournament and career. Taking the time to develop appropriate nutrition and hydration habits suitable for your child is well worth it as it is easy for them to fall into bad habits.

Actions to consider:

- Take nutrition for your child seriously – it can have a dramatic effect on their output.
- Spend time reviewing what your child currently eats and drinks.
- When shopping, make conscious choices about what to bring home.
- Add more low GI carbohydrates and good fats to the diet.
- Eliminate/reduce high GI carbohydrates and bad fats.
- Teach your child about hydration and ensure they rehydrate regularly.
- Build a consistent diet, including food and drink for your child before, during and after match play.
- Try not to let your child fall into bad habits.
- Readers are advised that they should seek medical advice before undertaking any specific diet or nutrition plans.

12
Building Mental Toughness

> Matches are won and lost so many times in the locker room.
> — Lleyton Hewitt, former world number one and winner of two grand slams, *The Daily Telegraph*, 2012

> I'm not afraid of anyone, but sometimes I'm afraid of myself. The mental part is very important.
> — Justine Henin, former world number one and winner of seven grand slams, *Sun Sports*, 2004

There is a cliché that 'sport is 90% mental, 10% physical', and in tennis this cliché holds true. Tennis certainly has to be one of the most challenging sports when it comes to the psychological pressure of competing in one-on-one situations. In team sports, a player's performance can often be hidden among their teammates or they make one particular contribution out of eleven, thirteen or fifteen players, while in tennis (singles) all the responsibility rests with the individual with no help from a coach (mid-match at least).

With tennis players being 100% accountable for their results, it is not surprising they display the full array of emotions, from elation and ecstasy when they're winning to getting extremely upset, throwing their racquet and crying on court when things aren't going their way. Tennis has a way of intensifying and bringing emotions to the surface, and players need the understanding and coping strategies to deal with these situations. Loss of control in this way can make the difference between winning and losing.

A lot of parents can see the importance of the mental side of tennis, yet the reality is few spend much time or many resources making sure their child is well equipped with the psychological foundations they need to be successful in elite tennis. It is hard to know where to start; it's hard to evaluate progress compared to other attributes such as technical or physical development.

This chapter outlines four important factors in improving the mental side of the game as well as providing tools and strategies to deal with this area. The four factors for having mental strength are a strong body, the ability to concentrate over long periods, the ability to deal with negative emotions, and maintaining motivation.

A strong body leads to a strong mind

According to psychologists, physical pain and emotional pain are located in the *same* area of the brain. What this means is that when players experience physical discomfort through training, they are making their brains stronger at coping with this type of pain, and because this part of the brain is largely responsible for coping with emotional pain too, being fitter physically means they're better equipped to cope with emotional discomfort. Physical training in many ways *is* mental training, and in most cases a player who is physically fitter than another will be mentally stronger in competition. This comes about for two reasons.

Players who are in great physical condition experience less physical discomfort on the court than those who are out of condition. When the players are in a long battle in a match, the fitter player will be more inclined to make smart decisions based on what will increase their chances of winning, while the unfit player will be likely to make their decisions based on how to reduce their physical pain. As a result, players who are experiencing physical discomfort tend to make a lot more unforced errors due to going for too much and trying to end the point too soon.

The second reason is that players who have conditioned themselves physically are used to pushing through the pain barriers and as a result are much better equipped to handle emotional discomfort as well. The more effectively players handle all the emotional challenges such as nerves and frustration, the better they will compete in important match situations.

One of the best activities a player can do to increase their mental toughness in general is to work hard on improving their physical condition, pushing themselves through barriers as often as possible.

> 'The stuff that Lleyton took to the top of the game – being prepared, being mentally tough, fighting every time – those are all things that you can teach someone and show someone, and he's the example I always use. I don't know that I could have more respect for Lleyton as a player.'[20]
> — Andy Roddick, former world number one and winner of one grand slam

Concentration – the ability to sustain constant pressure on opponents

The ability to concentrate over a long period of time is a vital skill for elite tennis players and it can often be the difference between a good and great player.

---

20 ABC News, 'Lleyton Hewitt in quotes' (2016) https://mobile.abc.net.au/news/2016-01-21/lleyton-hewitt-in-quotes/7093296?pfm=sm

In 2001, Lleyton Hewitt became the youngest ever player to achieve a world number one ranking on the men's ATP tour. Although Hewitt didn't have the typical weapons that his opponents had, he dominated the game when it came to sustaining constant point by point pressure over the duration of three- or five-set matches.

CASE STUDY – RYAN'S TWELVE-DAY EXPERIENCE WITH THE AUSTRALIAN DAVIS CUP TEAM

I was fortunate enough to be offered the opportunity to be the Orange Boy for the Davis Cup tie, held in Adelaide against India in 2002, which Lleyton Hewitt was a part of. I was seventeen years old.

The Orange Boy is an old tradition whereby up-and-coming players get the opportunity to spend time in the Davis Cup team environment and immerse themselves in the pre-training camp and event. In my case, it involved twelve days of sharing everything from practice, physical training, eating meals together with the team to supporting the team during the live matches. Lleyton Hewitt was the number one player in the world at the time and it was an unforgettable experience to practise and train with him. As a seventeen-year-old with an ATP world ranking of around 600, I was proud to be able to just keep up with Hewitt in drills and rally situations, but once we started playing full court points, it was a whole different ball game.

Hewitt rarely made an unforced error and ran me around from side to side almost every point, which was incredibly taxing physically and wore me down.

If we played first to eleven points from the baseline, I would be competitive for the first seven or eight points before I was out of breath, and he'd run away with the back half of the game. I had to keep in mind that this was only a first to eleven points, which was nothing compared to playing 100–200 points in a best of three-set match or 200+ points in a best of five-set match.

While Lleyton didn't serve or hit the ball as hard as other players I had competed against, he was by far the hardest to consistently win points against. His ability to play one tough point after another without lapses in concentration was a big reason why he became the youngest world number one male tennis player in history.

There are a number of key things that players can do to improve their point by point concentration and maintain a high level of play throughout an entire match:

Endurance. Fitness allows a player to put in 100% of their efforts for the full duration of a potentially long match. Players who are not in great physical condition may have good concentration skills, but will not be able to sustain their level of play for long periods when physical pain due to lack of endurance sets in.

Strategy focus. Players who are implementing a match strategy spend their time in between points reflecting on how the points are being won and lost and what to do next. A match strategy keeps players focused on the important detail in every point.

In-between-point routines. An effective in-between-point routine focuses on breathing, reflection and planning, and this will set the concentration tone for the point ahead. Players with poor routines in this area are often the ones to lose concentration. The next section outlines some steps your child can take in between points.

Work on concentration. Novak Djokovic is one of the professional players who practises working on his concentration every day. Concentration exercises using a meditation app can develop the skills to sustain concentration over long periods of time.

Having the ability to concentrate point by point over long periods of time requires a lot of practice, but it will make a huge difference to a player's progress over the long term.

Dealing with adversity and negative emotions

> The mark of great sportsmen is not how good they are at their best, but how good they are at their worst.
> — Martina Navratilova, former world number one and winner of eighteen grand slams

Tennis is an individual game with a unique scoring system that is seemingly designed to build pressure on both players, whether they're winning or losing.

Finding ways to deal with pressure and the resulting adversity is critical in a tennis player's development.

There is a common pattern in a lot of junior tennis matches:

- Stage 1: a player starts a match with a neutral mindset
- Stage 2: a player experiences adversity or a challenge of some kind
- Stage 3: the player experiences negative and difficult thoughts and emotions as a response to the adversity
- Stage 4: due to the discomfort of what the player is experiencing internally, their level of play drops off significantly

Tennis players at all levels of the game experience adversity of some sort when they are competing. Some common examples are:

- Opponent is cheating (or a player thinks he/she is cheating)
- Umpire has made a bad line call
- Fatigue and physical pain
- Not playing as well as expected
- Opponent is playing incredible tennis and is winning

Even top professional players are human and can experience strong negative thoughts and emotions when faced with challenges. The biggest difference between professionals and most junior players is they continue to take positive actions, regardless of what is going on internally. Most professionals know how to deal with their difficult emotions and have learned how to play well, however they are feeling.

The pro player's approach is:

- Stage 1: the professional player experiences adversity or a challenge of some kind
- Stage 2: they experience negative and difficult thoughts and emotions as a response to the adversity
- Stage 3: despite the discomfort of what they are experiencing internally, they continue to compete as hard as they possibly can to give themselves the best chance of winning and their level of play remains high

Negative emotions can be almost impossible to control at times and it's a lot easier to try and accept them. Mentally tough players learn how to take positive actions despite the emotions that they are experiencing, accepting that they are part of being human.

When your child is facing these challenges, here are some things they can do:

Be alert and mindful. Facing difficult challenges often brings up powerful emotions and feelings that can lead to a spiral of negative thinking. Once a player is in this downward spiral, it's difficult to break out of it. One of the keys to avoiding this is being mindful and alert when difficult thoughts and feelings arise and seeing them for what they are.

Take slow, deep breaths. Studies have shown that the way we breathe can have a big effect on our mindset. Short, shallow breaths tend to create panic, while slow, deep breathing creates calmness and clarity. A few deep breaths will go a long way to creating the clarity your child needs before taking the next crucial step.

Create an action plan and make decisions. If your child has followed steps 1 and 2, they should be ready to make a decision with clarity. Without calmness and clarity, decision making will usually be poor and lead to more adversity and problems.

Take action. After your child has made the decisions, they need to take action. Difficult thoughts and feelings may still be arising in their mind, but they need to learn to take positive action regardless. Top professional players also experience difficult thoughts and feelings, but they have trained themselves to take positive actions whatever they're feeling.

ReCAP

A quality in-between-point routine can help your child deal with negative emotions. A simple one that has worked for a lot of players is ReCAP:

Response. Did your child win or lose the point? In either case, they will have an instinctive response. Here are the best actions for them to take:

- Experiencing positive emotions: fist pump, shouting 'C'mon' when they've hit a great shot or won a long, critical point, or just look at their opponent to see how it affects them.

- Experiencing negative emotions: turn their back and walk away. The racquet is the barometer – your child always wants to keep their racquet head pointing up.

Compose. Take four or five deep breaths to calm down and avoid making potentially poor decisions in emotional state.

Assess. Your child needs to use their analytical skills to work out who is doing what to whom and how the points are being won and lost.

Plan and prepare. Your child needs to:

- Plan their upcoming point and what strategy they will be implementing based on the observations they have made in the previous step
- Prepare themselves physically and mentally by saying positive words to themselves such as target, compete or whatever inspires them, and moving their body (eg bouncing on their toes) to ensure they are ready for the upcoming point

In the Wimbledon quarter-finals in 2013, Andy Murray found himself down two sets to love against an in-form Fernando Verdasco. With Murray being an incredible competitor, he stayed in the moment and fought back point by point to eventually win the match in five sets; '… when you play more and more matches and gain more experience you understand how to turn matches around and how to change the momentum of games.'[21]

Andy was known to compete with great passion. He was often prone to experiencing intense negative emotions on the court, but had conditioned himself to compete hard and take positive action despite this.

Learning how to deal with adversity is one of life's core skills and tennis can be a great way to develop in this area.

---

21 Toby Davis, 'Murray fights back from the brink to sink Verdasco', *Reuters* (2013) www.reuters.com/article/us-tennis-wimbledon-murray/murray-comes-back-from-two-sets-down-to-beat-verdasco-idUSBRE96212J20130703

Maintaining motivation

It's never sacrifice when you love what you're doing.
— Stan Wawrinka, ATP Tour, 2019

The elite tennis journey can span several decades so it's critical for a player to maintain motivation over the long term. Below are some tips that will help players sustain and increase their motivation.

Set goals. It's important to have a written list of short-, medium- and long-term goals (see Chapter 4 for more details). Goal setting provides a compass for what to prioritise as well as seeing how your child is tracking, so include performance goals such as ranking/UTR while focusing on development areas such as technical, tactical, physiological and physical goals.

Measure progress. Personal growth is an important motivation factor, so periodically checking in to see how your child is tracking with their progress can help enormously. We've developed a series of tables using the UTR where your child can see what level of tennis they are tracking for now and in the future (see Chapter 4).

Celebrate milestones. Celebrating all the wins, no matter how small, whether it be achieving a particular ranking or rating or developing a certain aspect of the game, is vital to keep your child motivated in the long term. Tracking achievements helps to boost their confidence by activating the reward circuitry within their brain. This releases invigorating 'feel-good' chemicals like dopamine which fill them with a sense of accomplishment and pride.

Establish a positive peer group. Motivational speaker Jim Rohn says that we become the average of the five people we spend the most time with, and it's definitely true for tennis players. The reality is that high performers have different habits to low performers. High performers are generally more professional; work harder; have more attention to detail; are more committed; are more disciplined; have better nutrition; are goal oriented; are self-confident; and think bigger thoughts. The advantage of spending time with high performers is that these positive habits will rub off after a period of time.

One of the best ways for your child to increase motivation and improve their tennis in the long run is for them to become friends with players at a higher level and spend time in an environment where they all train together.

Visual exposure to a high level of tennis. The first section of Daniel Coyle's book *The Talent Code* talks about the positive effect on our brains and motivation when we watch high performers. Intensely watching a top-ranked junior or professional player train and compete can have a significant impact on short- and long-term motivation, and the more frequently your child is exposed to this, the greater effect it will have.

Some suggestions for your child are:

- At least once per year, go to professional ATP/WTA events to watch the pros train and play live matches. The closer you and your child can get to the court, the better.
- Watch the finals of nationals or big junior or open events that your child has competed in.
- Watch pro tennis on TV.
- Make sure your child regularly trains at a club or in an environment where there are like-minded elite players.
- Seek doubles partners for your child who play at a higher level.
- Subscribe to tennis magazines/YouTube channels.

Winning matches. Parents need to watch out for extended periods where their child is losing a high percentage of matches as this can have a negative effect on self-confidence and motivation. Typically, this occurs when players are entered in tournaments of a higher level than they are ready for. Make sure your child has a competition schedule that has them winning at least 50% of matches. If they lose in the early rounds for a couple of tournaments in a row, make sure they enter some events where they are likely to get wins on the board.

Summary

There are four key factors that deliver mental strength in tennis: a strong body, the ability to concentrate over long periods, the ability to deal with negative emotions, and maintaining motivation. Your child can develop all these areas through deliberate practice and adopting routines both before and during matches.

Actions to consider:

- Provide your child with the opportunity to build their fitness (strong body = strong mind).
- Develop their concentration by implementing structured routines.
- Provide them with the opportunity to learn coping strategies for dealing with adversity.
- Engage an expert who has experience in helping students with their psychology on the tennis court. An example is Mentally Tough Tennis www.mentallytoughtennis.com, a company with a successful track record of working with elite players, including professionals.
- Take action to make sure you child's motivation is maintained.

SECTION 4
WHERE CAN TENNIS LEAD?

From the beginning, I decided that if people came to me later on and told me that my daughters were great tennis players, I had failed. Success would be if they came up to me and said my daughters were great people.
— Richard Williams, father of Serena and Venus, *Black and White*, 2014

13
Becoming A Professional Tennis Player

> I think you need inspiration, motivation from different angles to keep you going, because it isn't that simple just to wake up every morning and go for another travel around the world, another practice... another stretch. It's always nice, but you need to have some success and you need to have the right reasons why you're doing it.
> — Roger Federer, ATP World Tour, 2012

A lot of young tennis players when they start getting involved in national ranking tournaments have the dream of travelling the world as a professional. This is a great goal to have as there will be many benefits for choosing this path, regardless of whether they achieve their goal.

Few players are ready to begin pursuing the professional pathway on graduating from high school, which is why the US college tennis option is fast becoming the most popular way to go for the world's best eighteen to twenty-two-year-old tennis players, both male and female. Below are some statistics that should encourage players to hold off pursuing the professional pathway until they've graduated from college.[22]

- The average age of players in the top 100 is twenty-eight for men and twenty-six for women.

- The average amount of time it takes from first professional tournament to breaking into the world's top 100 is four years.

- The number of players under the age of twenty inside the top 100 in 2018 was two men and four women.

The game has become a lot more physical than it was prior to the 1990s when many of the world's best players were in their early twenties. Players in today's game are playing much better tennis later in their careers and are not rushing to get on the tour. A good example of this is in late 2018, the male world number one, two and three (Nadal, Federer and Djokovic) were all over the age of thirty.

---

22 Tennis News, 'The numbers prove it: tennis players are getting older' (2018) https://tennishead.net/the-numbers-prove-it-tennis-players-are-getting-older

How good does your child need to be after high school to go pro?

Below are some guidelines that suggest your child may be ready to bypass college tennis and head straight on to the professional circuit after high school:

- Male players: UTR 14.75+ | Top 400 ATP | Top 5 ITF juniors

- Female players: UTR 12.75+ | Top 150 WTA | Top 5 ITF juniors

Justin Gimelstob, an American former professional, suggests parents should be able to answer yes to at least two of these three questions if their child is thinking of bypassing college tennis:[23]

1. Is your child able to compete at the highest levels, ie have they beaten players in the top 100?

2. Are they receiving a significant endorsement opportunity or some kind of financial incentive that they must take advantage of at this point to turn pro?

3. Would they dominate college tennis, ie would the competition just not be there?

---

23 Justin Gimelstob, 'Should You Go Pro Or Go To College?', *Tennis.com* (2018) http://baseline.tennis.com/article/71849/tennis-life-should-you-go-pro-or-go-college

Even if you can answer yes to all three, it is still a difficult decision to make due to how good the college experience is for both a player's tennis and academic studies, giving them a safety net if they don't achieve their pro-tennis aspirations.

The transition to pro tennis

When players are ready to make the transition to professional tennis, it's important they know what the levels are and how it all works. There are four tiers or levels of professional tennis:

Tier (1 being the best)	Name	Prize money	Approx. level Players	Approx. UTR
Tier 1	ATP/WTA tour including grand-slam events	US$250K–$50 million+	World's best/ top 100	Men: 15–16.5 Women: 12.65–13.4
Tier 2	Challenger/ ITF pro circuit	US$50K–$125K	World ranked 75–250	Men: 14.6–15.2 Women: 12.4–12.8
Tier 3	ITF pro circuit	US$25K+	World ranked 150–500	Men: 14.34–14.8 Women: 11.8–12.5
Tier 4	Transition tour	US$15K+	World ranked 400+	Men: 13.5–14.4 Women: 11–11.9

In 2019 the ITF reviewed the structure of the professional tour, however the principle will remain that players need to start at Tier 4 and work up to Tier 1.

Tennis is like most other professional sports in that there are no short cuts to being accepted into the highest levels of the game. As an example, for a player to move successfully from one tier to the next, they'll need to be able to beat most of the players in their current tier. The timeframe to move from Tier 4 to Tier 1 is around four years for the top 100 players, so it's important for players to be physically and mentally ready. Players who start the journey before they are ready often become discouraged and stop short of reaching their potential.

With the introduction of the UTR, a player can now compare their level to that of any player on the pro circuit to assess whether they will be able to compete at that level or not.

CASE STUDY – RYAN'S EXAMPLE

From 2000 to 2002 I was aggressively pursuing the international junior and professional circuit. While I had some success, finishing my last year of juniors inside the world top 20 and achieving an ATP world ranking of around 424 at the age of eighteen, there was never any suggestions from my coaches/mentors that I should consider the college pathway at any point.

I played several futures events, some challengers and a couple of pro-tour events, including the Australian Open, but the reality for me was that there was a huge difference between the level of the ITF world junior circuit and the professional circuit where I had to play against experienced professionals who were often more than ten years older than me.

When I was competing at the lowest level of professional tennis (Tier 4), I was making the occasional semi or final, but wasn't yet ready to break through and be a regular player at challenger or pro-tour events (Tier 3 and above). In reality, I needed a couple more years of development and improvement to increase my chances of being successful at the ATP tour, and in hindsight, college would have been the perfect solution.

As it turned out, repetitive injuries forced me into early retirement, but if I did it all over again, I would set my sights on the US college pathway. On the plus side, my experiences have helped shape the person I have become professionally and socially.

The business of professional tennis

Once a tennis player decides to become a professional, they are essentially trading as a small business. They derive their income from prize money (and endorsements for top players) and their expenses are mostly made up of flights, airport transfers, accommodation, food, restringing racquets, clothing and equipment.

> 'People think that there is so much money in tennis, but the reality is unless you're ranked in about the top 50 you don't earn much at all. It is hard to support yourself travelling the world, to be away from home most of the year

and to pay for a coach to help you become a better player.'[24]
— Samantha Stosur

Whether your child is successful in cracking the top 100 or not, professional tennis can be an incredible business experience for them if you set it up in the right way. This chapter aims to give you ideas on how to make your child self-supporting through this period while teaching them how the business world works.

Almost all professional tennis players start their journey without a timeline or clear plan and just play as long as they can until they run out of money or start getting injured. Before your child starts the professional tennis journey, you would be wise to create a plan upfront and answer the following questions:

- As a parent, how much money am I willing to invest?

- How much time is my child prepared to invest before they become self-supporting or profitable?

- When are the decision points going to be along the way if they are still losing money?

Being clear on a budget, timeline and decision points creates a sense of urgency for the player who values time and money.

---
24 Stosur, Samantha, 'Early tennis life is far from glamorous', *Herald Sun* (2013) www.heraldsun.com.au/sport/tennis/samantha-stosur-early-tennis-life-is-far-from-glamorous/news-story/4eefb9f339432c4d82df d5511d3d6286

Income

Below is a breakdown of the average amount players earn in prize money in each ranking bracket of the top 200 (from January to July 2019).[25]

- 1–25: US$ 2,245,787
- 26–50: US$ 824,861
- 51–75: US$ 598,440
- 76–100: US$ 448,158
- 101–125: US$ 344,052
- 126–150: US$ 256,116
- 151–175: US$ 169,154
- 176–200: US$ 131,629

Expenses

On average it costs a tennis player US$38,800 per year to travel, sleep and eat on tour, and that's not factoring in the cost of a coach. According to the same research, which was conducted in 2014 by the ITF, the break-even ranking in the men's game is **No 336 in the world**, and for women **No 253**.[26] This sounds

---

25 ATP World Tour, 'ATP Prize Money Leaders (US$)' (2019) www.protennislive.com/posting/ramr/current_prize.pdf
26 ITF World Tennis tour, 'Player Pathway Review' (2017) www.itftennis.com/procircuit/about-itf-world-tennis-tour/player-pathway.aspx

reasonable until you consider that, at that time, there were nearly 9,000 male players and more than 2,000 women professionals swinging a racquet.

Beyond breaking even, consider the amount of investment income that a player requires for retirement. If a player retires at thirty years old, owns a house and has $1 million worth of investment assets, this will only last until they're forty-two with an average 5% return on investment if they're spending $100K per annum. This is why it is important for your child to have a long-term view on their career and managing finances for life.

Doubles as a way to build a tennis career

Singles is the glamorous side of tennis, but doubles, along with being a highly enjoyable game, is an important means to build a player's income, particularly as they start out.

CASE STUDY - JOHN PEERS'S EXAMPLE

The Australian player John Peers understood the business component better than most tennis players. In 2011, when Peers decided to embark on a professional tennis career, he was two years into a finance degree at a US college and had a business plan.

His plan was simple. He set himself two years to be self-sustainable (income higher than expenses) and judged that breaking into the world's top 100 singles ranking was a distant prospect, but he had the game style to establish himself as a top 50 doubles player where he could make a good rather than spectacular living. He reached that goal in 2013 and is now half of one of the world's best doubles teams. He's also among Australia's most financially successful tennis players with over US$3.4 million in prize money as of 2019.

Peers commented, 'I came out of college and gave myself two years to become financially independent, otherwise I would have gone back to uni, finished my degree and gone back to the workforce. I studied finance and thought that, at the end of two years, if I couldn't make it in two years, I'd choose another profession.

'You can't make money from futures and challengers (tours for players ranked outside the top 100). For me it was about trying to get into the biggest events as quickly as possible. The best opportunity I had was through doubles. From a business standpoint, it was a very smart decision.'

CASE STUDY – LUKE'S EXAMPLE

Doubles was great for my confidence as a player in general. Although my main focus was always on singles, my game style was well suited to doubles. Throughout my career I had wins over players such as David Ferrer, Mardy Fish and the Bryan Brothers, which also made me more confident in singles.

One of the other major benefits of playing doubles on the professional tour was the ability to earn prize money when I was knocked out of the singles event. Often this would be the difference between making a loss or profit for that week.

US college provides a platform for going pro

A player who has just graduated from high school will usually be playing at a level that is a long way off their potential and a long way from being able to compete on the professional tour. To have any chance of being successful on the ATP or WTA tour, players will need to have the following UTR as a minimum when they're starting at the lowest rungs of professional tennis:

- Male players: 13.75+
- Female players: 11.5+

This is a high bar for an eighteen-year-old straight out of high school. Contrast this with, as an example, a male player who goes to college with a UTR of 11.5. He will have four years to get his UTR up to 13.75+.

As of 2019, these UTRs put a player at a level of around 800 in the world. This means that when they begin competing on the transitional tour, they'll be at a similar level to the players they'll be competing against and can make the transition to bigger events as they further develop and improve.

Below is an example of a business plan for a player who has just graduated from high school with a decent playing level and a limited budget. This example is for a male player, but it can just as easily be applied to a female player.

Let's assume that the player's parents have set up an account for their son with US$50,000 and that he will be self-supporting from the age of eighteen onwards with his parents not contributing financially to his tennis thereafter. Once the $50,000 is gone, if their son isn't earning enough from tennis to be self-supporting, it's time for him to pursue a career outside of professional tennis.

This scenario is a particularly powerful motivator and has worked for many current players on the tour as they realise the value of time and money at a much younger age.

Assumptions:

- Male player, age eighteen
- UTR: 11.75
- Budget to spend on pro-tennis career: US$50,000

Phase 1: age eighteen to twenty-two (four years)

Main goals:

- To achieve a UTR of 13.75 or higher by university graduation to be ready for the transitional ITF pro circuit events
- To break even or build bank balance over this period

Expenses	Details
Training	Included in college programme
Match play	US college tennis/European club tennis in college off season
Physical development	Included in college programme
Sport psychology	Included in college programme
Nutrition plan	Included in college programme
Travel expenses	Mostly covered by college tennis
Restringing	Mostly covered by college
Clothing and equipment	Mostly covered by college
Accommodation	Included in college programme
Shortfall	With an 85%+ scholarship, we'll assume an average loss of US$10,000 per year

The US college tennis season goes on for approximately eight and a half months of the year. This leaves three and a half months of the year for the player to continue to develop his tennis while building up a bank balance at the same time.

Income	How
Coaching	Most tennis clubs are always on the lookout for good coaches. When players return home, they can offer their services as a part-time tennis coach over the college holiday period.
Restringing	This is a great skill to have to earn additional income anywhere in the world all year round.

Continued

European club tennis	Many clubs in Europe are always on the lookout for good players to compete in their teams. During the college off season, a player could find an arrangement where they get all their expenses covered and get a fee for each match they play. This can be a great way to develop as a player and build up the bank balance.
Surplus	Aiming for US$10,000 per year or to at least match yearly expenses.

Checkpoint 1 (age twenty-two/twenty-three, after college graduation):

If at the end of college, the player's UTR is not around 13.75, going pro will be difficult and expensive. He could travel around to events and compete, but his level of success will likely be limited unless he can quickly develop his game. The decision at this point is to either pursue the professional circuit or take steps to begin a working career.

Phase 2: age twenty-two to twenty-four (two years)

The player has now graduated from college and is out in the real world, beginning the journey of professional tennis if he has achieved his graduation UTR goal. This two-year period is a crucial stage where most players will end their journey. With a limited budget, they will be doing this stage on their own or with a part-time coach to help them when they're back at the training base at home.

Main goals:

- To achieve a UTR of 15+ to break into the world's top 200
- To keep a bank balance alive and reinvest surplus funds back into development such as hiring a part-time travelling coach

Expenses	Details
Training	Done on the road at tournaments with other professional players or at home in a training block.
Match play	Entry fees paid at professional events.
Physical development	Paid-for programme designed by professional trainer which the player can implement in gyms when travelling.
Sport psychology	Assume by this stage the player has good foundations and is not investing in this area.
Nutrition plan	Paid-for individualised nutrition plan designed by a sports dietitian to implement fifty-two weeks of the year.
Travel expenses	Flights, airport transfers.
Clothing and equipment	Shoes, strings and racquets.
Restringing	Restringing costs can become expensive, which is why travelling with a small restringing machine can save lots of money and potentially be an income stream.
Accommodation	Hotels etc.
Shortfall	Estimated shortfall is $38,800 according to Tennis Australia and ITF research.

Income	How
Prize money	The more he progresses in tournaments, the more money the player will make.
European club tennis	Many clubs in Europe are always on the lookout for good players to compete in their teams. This can be a great way to develop as a player and build up the bank balance.
Coaching	Most tennis clubs are always on the lookout for good coaches.
Restringing	This is a great skill to have to earn additional income.
Surplus	Aiming for US$10,000 per year or to at least match yearly expenses.

Checkpoint 2 (after two years of competing on the professional circuit):

If the player has no money left, he has two options:

- Stop pursuing professional tennis and start a career.

- Raise additional capital and continue the journey. We would only recommend this if he is still improving or feels he has a lot of upside left in his game.

If he still has money in the bank, the player's dream is alive. If he is top 200, he can move up to the next phase. If he is not, he can consider the following options:

- If his game is still improving, he can continue doing what he is doing.
- He can stop and take whatever money he has to either give back to his parents or use in another way.

Phase 3:

If all goes to plan and the player in our example is now in the top 200 in the world, he should be starting to make a profit. He may be tempted to bank it at this stage, but this is where he needs to reinvest profits into his development, perhaps getting a full-time travelling coach and doing whatever it takes to crack the world top 50. Once he's inside the world top 50, he can easily pay for all the support services he'll need to stay there.

Hopefully this example has given you a rough idea on how to create the framework of a business plan for your son or daughter.

CASE STUDY – RYAN'S EXAMPLE

I was fortunate enough at the age of eighteen to play in the Australian Open men's singles and doubles in 2003. I lost the first round of singles but won a round in the doubles before losing to the number one team in the world.

This was the biggest pay cheque I had ever received, and after taxes and AIS deductions, I netted around

$18,000. As an eighteen-year-old, I found this almost too good to be true, and having no understanding of business at the time, the first thing I did was go out and spend $3,000 on a kite surfing kit. If I had been smarter, I would have saved it towards future tournaments, travel and coaching expenses.

Summary

As with any further-education or career decision, you and your child need to give serious time and consideration to budgeting and planning. This will help your son or daughter understand how to pursue professional tennis as a career. While it can be a rewarding path, there are many pitfalls, so take the time to understand these and navigate your child's way around them.

Actions to consider:

- Understand the level and commitment your child requires to be a professional tennis player.

- When your child has graduated from high school (or when they are ready), create a plan that involves a budget and timeline for decision points.

- If your child is achieving success, encourage them to reinvest their money back into their own tennis career so they can break into the world's top 100.

14
Life After Professional Tennis

> The power of positive thinking really helped me in my career. It's important to remember that opportunities arise from setbacks. If you can show your boss that you can stay positive in the face of adversity, that is very powerful.
> — Pat Rafter, Australian Institute of Business, 2017

When your son or daughter approaches the end of their tennis career, if they have balanced tennis with a university education and built a strong network within the sport of friends and aficionados, they will be well placed and there will be many options for them to pursue. As tennis is a successful and growing international business, there are more and more attractive careers within the sport. Outside of tennis, players who have a background in elite-level sport, a strong character and a university education will always be attractive to future employers.

The character traits that tennis gives young players provide them with an amazing advantage over people who have not played competitive sport to a high level. These traits include training discipline, the continual learning and development approach, competitiveness, and the ability to solve problems on their feet and deal with adversity, and they are incredibly valuable.

There are two options for tennis players when they're considering what to do with their working career:

- Use their education and life experiences to pursue a career in any field
- Pursue a career in the tennis industry

This chapter provides several examples of people who have achieved success in their careers after tennis.

Pursuing a career outside of tennis

One area that tennis players seem to do well in is the finance industry. Earlier in the book, we shared the case study of Jeremy Bourgeois and how his tennis helped him get a great job with Macquarie Bank. An article published in www.businessinsider.com.au

entitled '53 Of The Most Serious Tennis Players In Finance' talks about the amount of tennis players who are using their competitive nature to achieve success on Wall Street in New York. These former players do well in this industry primarily because of their ambition and ability to set goals and achieve them.

New York Investment Banker Jeffrey Appel said:

> 'Many firms like to hire Ivy League athletes because if somebody was able to be a good student while also playing a sport it shows they have discipline and a competitive drive in addition to being intelligent and are able to balance multiple challenges at the same time, which gives them a higher probability of success in the competitive world of Wall Street.'[27]

Wall Street is littered with tennis players, many of them former top-ranked juniors. Some were All-Americans in college and some played professionally and were ranked globally, doing business around their forehands and backhands. On Wall Street, they know each other well and feel comfortable doing business together. A lot of the younger players meet their future employers on the court, and certain firms just love tennis players in general.

---

27   Julia La Roche, 'You Can Find Wall Street's Biggest Titans On The Tennis Courts On Sunday Morning', *New York Investment Banker* (2014) www.businessinsider.com.au/wall-street-tennis-community-2014-10

And it's not just the finance sector that tennis players are having success in.

CASE STUDY – WAYNE PASCOE

Wayne grew up in Adelaide and became South Australia's top-ranked player at twenty years of age while studying economics at the University of Adelaide. In 1979, after completing his degree and working as an accountant for two years, Wayne decided to back himself and, at the age of twenty-four, took up professional tennis as a new career. He travelled with John Fitzgerald for his initial two years, reached the last sixteen in doubles at Wimbledon in 1981, played in the main draw of all grand slams except for the French, playing tournaments in Europe, America and Asia.

After four years of professional tennis, Wayne returned to business, obtained a second degree in marketing and built a successful career in commercial property, working for eleven years with Colliers International as both an Australian director and Philippines managing director before running his own advisory business for the last nineteen years.

Wayne Pascoe has never lost his passion for playing and now competes on the world senior circuit whenever time allows. He has claimed several national seniors titles, reaching a high of number four in the world for his age group, and in 2018, he was part of the Australian team to win the world title for the over sixties.

Wayne continues to mix sport with business, running a successful Australia-wide commercial property advisory company, playing tennis as often as possible and giving back to the sport by serving on the board of Tennis NSW from 2011 to 2018, including being appointed president in his last year.

This is what Wayne has to say about tennis:

'Tennis has helped me in both sport and business by teaching me how to give your best, whether you win or lose. It has opened many doors in life, kept me fit and given me a challenge for life – to be the world over-85s singles champ!'

CASE STUDY – MARK LESCHLY

Business career: founder and managing partner of Iconica Partners (www.iconicapartners.com), a principal firm investing at the interface of sports, media and technology. Mark is an owner in several sports teams and leagues including the Los Angeles Football Club (Major League soccer team in LA), Professional Fighters League (a new mixed martial arts league), Team Liquid (e-sports) and Oklahoma City Dodgers (AAA Minor League baseball team). He is also an owner and managing partner of Rho Capital Partners, a leading technology-focused venture capital and private equity firm with over $2.5 billion under management (www.rho.com). In 2018, Mark also became the principal owner, chairman and CEO of Universal Tennis which is taking the tennis world by storm with a game-changing rating system that is now in more than 200 countries.

Education: graduated from Harvard University with a BA with honours and received an MBA from Stanford University's Graduate School of Business.

Tennis background: Mark was born in Denmark and was a highly ranked junior player, achieving a career-high ATP world ranking of 486. He was also selected for the Danish Davis Cup team. His high level of tennis allowed him to be accepted on to the Harvard University Tennis team where he became captain and number one player. Mark is a member of the United States Tennis Association (USTA) Foundation Advisory Board and USTA Player Development Council.

Pursuing a career in tennis

A lot of players who reach the elite levels of the game have been heavily committed to tennis their whole life. They have extensive knowledge of the game, love tennis and can add a lot of value to the industry. Being involved in an industry that they are passionate about makes work seem like fun, particularly when they are surrounded by like-minded people.

Worldwide there are well over 100,000 people pursuing full-time careers in tennis in a variety of ways. Some of the world's largest tennis employers' areas:

- Tennis federations such as the ATP, WTA, ITF
- National governing bodies like the USTA or Tennis Australia
- Television channels
- Tennis academies and clubs

- High schools
- Colleges
- Player management groups
- Tennis equipment manufacturers
- Tennis court construction companies

These organisations need talented professionals and executives in areas such as marketing, sales, sponsorship, public relations, membership, management, publishing, business operations, finance and accounting, legal, human resources, live commentating, customer service, court construction, facility design, engineering, information systems, information technology, web design, manufacturing, journalism, research and development, retail/pro shop, physical training, sports medicine, psychology and college placement. Below is an example of someone who has been successful in pursuing a corporate career in tennis.

CASE STUDY – CRAIG TILEY

Working career: Craig began his working career as a professional tennis coach in South Africa and then the United States. As a US college coach his teams set numerous records in winning national titles. Craig was awarded US National Coach of the Year twice. He also served as captain of the South African Davis Cup Team and coached several top professional players. After over fifteen years in coaching, Craig accepted a position with Tennis Australia to serve as its director of player development. He then progressed through the organisation and is now the CEO and the tournament director of the Australian Open, which is regarded as one of the best-run sporting events in the world.

Education: upon graduating from high school, Craig attended Stellenbosch University in South Africa followed by Tyler Junior College in Texas, and the University of Texas (Tyler) and graduated with a bachelor's degree in economics and a master's degree in kinesiology.

Tennis history: Craig was born in Durban, South Africa, and started playing tennis at the age of twelve, becoming a top-ranked junior. He played college tennis for Stellenbosch University and competed in lower tier professional events for a couple of years.

Tennis coaching – a career with potential

As with any industry, skilled people will be invaluable to tennis, and skilled coaches will have a world of opportunity. There is a shortage of high-quality tennis professionals in Australia and around the world, which is great news for those looking to pursue this pathway.

Here are two examples of coaches who have experienced joy and success in pursuing a career in tennis.

CASE STUDY – GLENN BUSBY

Coaching career: Glenn started coaching in his teens, and after completing his studies, he moved to the United States for two years and coached at a tennis academy in Florida where he advanced his career as a tennis coach.

Shortly after he relocated back to Australia, he started his own academy before getting the incredible opportunity to work at Kooyong (the former site of the Australian Open), which is one of the world's best tennis clubs with around 9,000 members and fifty-three tennis courts. He's been the director of tennis there for over twenty years and has a team of more than twenty-five coaches working under him.

Education: after graduating from high school, he achieved university degrees in physical education and biology.

Tennis history: Glenn was one of Australia's best juniors growing up in Melbourne. He won the Australian Open junior doubles title in 1975 and reached the semi-final of the singles. He played on the professional circuit in his spare time throughout university and achieved a career-high ATP world ranking of 326.

When he's not running his tennis academy at Kooyong, Glenn enjoys travelling the world competing on the ITF senior circuit, in which he's had a lot of success, being world number one for his age group for twelve of the past fourteen years, winning fourteen world championships (seven singles titles, five team and two doubles titles). Glenn loves travelling with his mates on the senior circuit:

'Seniors for a lot of people fulfils something they couldn't do when they were younger for whatever reason. I know it has for me. It's... allowed me to have that competitiveness while still having a business and... wanting to train and work with young players. It's a good blend all the way through. For me it's not about money, but enjoyment and experiences... which is lacking in some of our Australian players.'

CASE STUDY – PETER BURWASH

Recognised as one of the game's top coaches, Peter has served as a keynote speaker at tennis conferences, an instruction editor and contributor for *Tennis* magazine and other international publications, and as a television commentator for TSN and CBC. He has authored ten books, including *Tennis For Life*, which is an industry best seller. He is the recipient of numerous awards and been inducted into the Tennis Industry Hall of Fame, as well as the USPTA Hall of Fame.

Tennis history: as a player in Canada, Peter was a top-ranked junior, Canadian university champion, and is a former Canadian number one and Davis Cup player. Through this period, Peter discovered he loved coaching as much as playing tennis. After graduating, Peter competed professionally on the international circuit, and continued to conduct tennis clinics wherever he travelled. After six years on the tour, he had played and coached in over 100 countries.

Working career: upon retiring from professional tennis in 1975, Peter wanted to offer others the opportunities to travel and share the gift of tennis that he had experienced. He founded Peter Burwash International –

one of the world's most successful tennis management companies which currently operates the tennis programme at fifty-nine first-class resorts and clubs in over twenty-four countries.

Education: Peter earned a Bachelor of Physical and Health Education degree from the University of Toronto, Canada.

Peter is a huge believer in the benefits of tennis:

'Tennis teaches you all the important things, all the things you need to know. It teaches you to stand on your own, to be patient, to know that there are going to be losses, and to learn from those losses. From tennis, you learn that you're not going to have a good day every day. It also teaches you to change directions because life is not a straight path. It teaches you to ask yourself, "What can I try next because this isn't working?"'

There are many examples of people just like Glenn and Peter who have achieved success and fulfilment through pursuing a career they are passionate about. We will end by sharing our insights into our own working careers. While our business, Voyager, is in its infancy compared to some of those we've described in this chapter, it has already given us huge pleasure alongside the opportunity to impart our passion and love for tennis.

CASE STUDY – RYAN'S EXAMPLE

I retired from tennis at the age of twenty and my best decision was to stay involved in the game. My first job was coaching at Tennis NSW, working under some incredible coaches and mentors such as Graeme Brimblecombe and Wally Masur. My job there was to coach some of the best junior players in Australia, and during that time I was fortunate enough to work with players who eventually reached the top.

After four years' experience at Tennis NSW, I gained another four years' experience on the club coaching scene (coaching players of all ages and abilities) in London and Sydney, before co-founding Voyager Tennis Academy in 2011 with Luke, who specialises in the development of elite players.

Building a business from scratch has been an incredible personal development journey for me and has presented many challenges and opportunities. I've had to learn business fundamentals such as building a team, creating a culture, management, marketing, finance, administration, creating partnerships and many other skills that I didn't know anything about when I finished playing on the circuit. I've had the opportunity to present at the Grand Slam Coaches' Conference at the Australian Open, and now I'm an author of a book. I was also elected to be a director on the Tennis NSW Board in 2017, which is allowing me to give back to the tennis industry as well as gain boardroom experience and an understanding of how tennis operates on a macro level.

Perhaps the most enjoyable part of my career in tennis has been the opportunity to work alongside some of my good mates every day, many of whom I played against right back to the 10/U days, which is priceless and makes my professional career a fun experience.

CASE STUDY – LUKE'S EXAMPLE

Unlike Ryan, I spent my twenties playing on the professional circuit until I retired in 2007 at the age of thirty. My wealth of experience on the pro tour and travelling with Roger Federer fuelled a passion in me to coach and mentor up-and-coming elite junior and senior players.

When I finished my playing career, I relocated back to Sydney and began coaching a bunch of Sydney's best players, many of whom have now gone on to achieve scholarships at world class US colleges or play on the professional circuit. A couple of years later I co-founded Voyager with Ryan and have been able to continue my passion for working with elite junior players in my role within the business. I am the director of tennis at our main site at Sydney Olympic Park.

In the last couple of years, I've won the Newcombe Medal for the Talent Development Coach of the Year in Australia, and Voyager has won the Tennis NSW Tennis School of the Year Award for its programme at Sydney Olympic Park. The transition from a player to a business owner has been a great journey for me. There have been many challenges, but the grit that I developed throughout my tennis career has allowed me to keep moving forward. I also love working in a high-performance environment around close mates, which makes my working life that much more enjoyable.

> The great thing about pursuing a tennis career is that you can get involved in whatever you are most passionate about, whether that be coaching kids or adults, working with elite players, officiating, or running a business, tournaments and events. All the opportunities are available if you work hard and are patient.

Summary

Tennis is a wonderful platform to launch a career from – the examples of the men and women in this chapter who have great careers with tennis as a foundation are testament to that. Tennis develops human qualities, a competitive instinct and a formidable and invaluable network. Combining competitive tennis with a university education is an incredible opportunity that we strongly encourage our students to consider. Tennis for both of us has been a life-enhancing voyage, and we believe that it has the potential to be an incredible springboard for children's lives.

We hope that this book has given you and your child an overview of the journey involved in becoming an elite player, inspiration about the education and career opportunities that tennis can provide, details about the development areas that you need to consider and some insight into the key role that parents play.

We wish you and your child all the best with your tennis voyage.

Acknowledgements

We wrote this book ultimately because we love the game of tennis and want others to enjoy and get as much from it as we have done and continue to do. We would like to acknowledge the people who have contributed towards enabling us to play, enjoy and make careers from tennis.

Parents and extended family have always been there to provide unconditional support, resources and transportation to all our thousands of hours of training and competition. They have been by far the biggest influence on our tennis careers and enjoyment of the game.

Our coaches have contributed by being passionate, knowledgeable and nurturing, and have been responsible for keeping us intrigued and excited about tennis.

Our tennis mates have made the whole journey rewarding with lots of fun, some mischief, sharing highs and lows together, and the development of great friendships.

The governing bodies of our sport have made it all possible, for without them, the game would not exist in the same way. We've been fortunate enough to have travelled to countries all over the world, some places barely having a decent tennis court to play on or any coaching or competition structure, so we realise how lucky we are to have a developed tennis infrastructure in Australia and a thriving governing body that is investing in the game at all levels.

This book has involved a lot of sacrifices, so we would like to thank:

Our wives and children for being supportive throughout the writing of this book, allowing us to sacrifice family time on evenings, weekends and holidays.

The Voyager Tennis Academy team for providing incredible input and living every day as role models to the young tennis players who look up to them.

Our partners Study and Play USA, Precision Athletica, The McDonald College and Mentally Tough Tennis for helping bring together a holistic philosophy that produces not only great players, but well-rounded people as well. A special thanks to Dr Anthony Ross

ACKNOWLEDGEMENTS

who is an inspiration and has provided input and shaped our thinking around best-practice sports psychology for tennis players.

George Wheen, tennis parent of an elite player himself, who has been an incredible mentor, client and friend over the past couple of years, providing invaluable input and guidance to bring this book together. George, you have been the most pivotal person in helping prepare this book for publishing and we'd like to make this special note to thank you.

Finally, we'd like to acknowledge the passing of Todd Reid at the young age of thirty-four. Todd was an incredible player and great friend who played a pivotal role in both of our tennis journeys, particularly Ryan's from age ten onwards. He will always be remembered for his spirit, friendship, competitive battles on the court and all the fun times we had.

RIP, Reidy.

References

ABC News, 'Lleyton Hewitt in quotes' (2016) https://mobile.abc.net.au/news/2016-01-21/lleyton-hewitt-in-quotes/7093296?pfm=sm

Agassi, A., *Open: An Autobiography* (Harper Collins, 2010)

ATP World Tour, 'ATP Prize Money Leaders (US$)' (2019) www.protennislive.com/posting/ramr/current_prize.pdf

Auerbach, N., 'In changeover, Venus asks the questions', *USA Today* (2010). View article title at www.pressreader.com

Australian Institute of Business, 'Tennis legend Pat Rafter shares his secrets for success at AIB Graduation' (2017) www.aib.edu.au/blog/news/pat-rafter-aib-graduation

Cassidy J., and Shaver P. R., *Handbook of Attachment: Theory, Research, and Clinical Applications* (Guildford Press, 2018) Craddock, R., 'Lleyton Hewitt talks footy dreams and on-court rivalries ahead of the Brisbane International', *The Daily Telegraph* (2012)

CEO Magazine, 'A look at the link between playing sports and success in business' (2018) www.theceomagazine.com/business/management-leadership/look-link-playing-sports-success-business

Clarey, C. 'The Secret to Roger Federer's Success is This Man' (2017) www.nytimes.com/2017/11/12/sports/tennis/roger-federer-atp-finals.html

College Scholarships, 'Tennis Scholarships For Your College Education', www.collegescholarships.org/scholarships/sports/tennis.htm

Cronin, M., 'Federer On His One-Hander: It all starts with the footwork', *Tennis.com* (2014) www.tennis.com/pro-game/2014/01/federer-his-one-hander-it-all-starts-footwork/50327

D'Angelo Friedman, J., 'My Healthy SELF: Defending US Open Champ Sam Stosur

REFERENCES

Reveals Her Favorite Tennis-Inspired Workout Moves', *Self* (2012) www.self.com/story/my-healthyself-tennis-champ-sa

Davis, T., 'Murray fights back from the brink to sink Verdasco' (2013) https://uk.reuters.com/article/uk-tennis-wimbledon-murray/murray-fights-back-from-the-brink-to-sink-verdasco-idUKBRE96212N20130703

Dickens, M., 'Martina Navratilova: Three Decades Of Tennis Excellence, A Lifetime Of Standing Up And Speaking Out' (2018) www.tennis-tourtalk.com/39322/martina-navratilova-three-decades-of-tennis-excellence-a-lifetime-of-standing-up-and-speaking-out

Eccleshare, C., 'Farewell Martina Hingis – a retrospective of tennis's great survivor', *The Telegraph* (2017) www.telegraph.co.uk/tennis/2017/10/27/farewell-martina-hingis-appreciation-tenniss-great-survivor

Elkins, K., 'These 9 successful CEOs all played sports in college' (2015) www.businessinsider.com.au/successful-ceos-who-played-sports-in-college-2015-2?r=US&IR=T#ge-ceo-jeffrey-immelt-played-football-for-dartmouth-1

Federer, R., Facebook, NikeCourt, Lessons From The Court (2013) www.facebook.com/nikecourt/photos/

lessons-from-the-court-2013-roger-federertennis-can-be-a-very-frustrating-sport-/10153565733650332

Federer, R., 'Federer Inspired By Love For The Game', ATP World Tour (2012) https://en.wikiquote.org/wiki/Roger_Federer

Giampaolo, F., *The Tennis Parent's Bible: Second Edition* (CreateSpace Independent Publishing Platform, 2016)

Gimelstob, J., 'Should You Go Pro Or Go To College?' (2018) http://baseline.tennis.com/article/71849/tennis-life-should-you-go-pro-or-go-college

Gray, D., 'When Jayne met Roger: How tennis legend inspired new a2 Milk boss' (2018) www.smh.com.au/business/companies/when-jayne-met-roger-how-tennis-legend-inspired-new-a2-milk-boss-20180731-p4zupe.html

Gutierrez, V., 'Now It's Serena's Turn to Take Title', *Los Angeles Times* (2000) www.latimes.com/archives/la-xpm-2000-aug-14-sp-4067-story.html

Hanna, C., 'A university degree is worth $1,180,112 over the course of a lifetime' (2017) www.smh.com.au/money/a-university-degree-is-worth-1180112-over-the-course-of-a-lifetime-20171026-gz8mgd.html

Hingis, M., 'Martina Hingis: My Mom', *Tennis.com* (2015) www.tennis.com/pro-game/2015/12/martina-hingis-my-mother/56922

REFERENCES

ITF World Tennis tour, 'Player Pathway Review' (2017) www.itftennis.com/procircuit/about-itf-world-tennis-tour/player-pathway.aspx

Jago, R., 'Federer's mental powers keep record in sight', *The Guardian* (2007) www.theguardian.com/sport/2007/mar/05/tennis.sport

La Roche, J., 'You Can Find Wall Street's Biggest Titans On The Tennis Courts On Sunday Morning' (2014) www.businessinsider.com.au/wall-street-tennis-community-2014-10

Leand, A. *ATP Insider* (2002) www.rediff.com/sports/2002/feb/12atp.htm

McCormack, M. H., *What They Don't Teach You at Harvard Business School* (Profile Books, 2014)

McGaugh, J. L., 'The Amygdala Modulates the Consolidation of Memories of Emotionally Arousing Experiences' *Annual Review of Neuroscience* (2004) www.annualreviews.org/doi/abs/10.1146/annurev.neuro.27.070203.144157

McGuire, K., 'NCAA revenue jumps closer to $1 billion' (2015) http://collegefootballtalk.nbcsports.com/2015/03/11/ncaa-revenue-jumps-closer-to-1-billion

McRae, D., 'Rafael Nadal: For everybody there are tough moments. This year, mine came', *The Guardian* (2009) www.theguardian.com/sport/2009/nov/17/rafael-nadal-interview-atp-world-tour-finals

Meah, A., '45 Inspirational Roger Federer Quotes on Success', *Awaken the Greatness Within* www.awakenthegreatnesswithin.com/45-inspirational-roger-federer-quotes-on-success

Morales, M., 'Stanislas Wawrinka: Tennis' Swiss Powerhouse Aims to Beat the Best', *Forbes* (2014) www.forbes.com/sites/miguelmorales/2014/01/18/stanislas-wawrinka-tennis-swiss-powerhouse-aims-to-beat-the-best/#5f551d632d5e

Nadal, R., and Carlin, J., *Rafa* (Hachette Books, 2011)

Nadal, R., Twitter, US Open Tennis (2018) https://twitter.com/usopen/status/1028091754589966336

Newcomb, T., *'Beyond the Bounce' (2015)* www.si.com/tennis/2015/10/14/tennis-balls-atp-wta-matches

Newman, P., 'Revealed: The diet that saved Novak Djokovic' (2013) www.frasercoastchronicle.com.au/news/revealed-diet-saved-novak-djokovic/1992684

NewsMail (2017) www.pressreader.com/australia/newsmail/20170926/page/21

REFERENCES

Pye, J., 'Henin-Hardenne slams it home', *Sun Sports* (2004) https://products.kitsapsun.com/archive/2004/01-31/389943_henin-hardenne_slams_it_home.html

Ramachandran, N., 'Q&A with the Bryan Brothers, tennis' best duo', *The Stanford Daily* (2016) www.stanforddaily.com/2016/05/28/de-nr-qa-with-the-bryan-brothers

Rich, B., 'The 25 Highest-Paid College Coaches of 2019', The Quad (2019) https://thebestschools.org/magazine/highest-paid-college-coaches

Saini, M., 'Venus Williams: A Force Off The Court' (2010) www.forbes.com/sites/face-to-face/2010/08/02/venus-williams-a-force-off-the-court/#21898a04c55a

Selhub, E., 'Nutritional psychiatry: Your brain on food' (2018) www.health.harvard.edu/blog/nutritional-psychiatry-your-brain-on-food-201511168626

Siegel, A., *Finding Your Own Fountain of Youth: The Essential Guide to Maximizing Health* (Paul Mould Publishing, 2008)

Smith, C., 'College Football's Most Valuable Teams' (2018) www.forbes.com/sites/chrissmith/2018/09/11/college-footballs-most-valuable-teams

Sprecher, M. H., 'Peter Burwash: Life lessons from tennis', Tennis Industry Magazine (2010) www.tennisindustrymag.com/articles/2010/08/21_peter_burwash.html

Stosur, S., 'Early tennis life is far from glamorous', News Corp Australia Network (2013) www.heraldsun.com.au/sport/tennis/samantha-stosur-early-tennis-life-is-far-from-glamorous/news-story/4eefb9f339432c4d82dfd5511d3d6286

Syed, M., *Bounce: The Myth of Talent and the Power of Practice* (New York: HarperCollins, 2010)

Tennis News, 'The numbers prove it: tennis players are getting older' (2018) https://tennishead.net/the-numbers-prove-it-tennis-players-are-getting-older

Tracy, B., 'Successful People Are Self Disciplined' www.briantracy.com/blog/time-management/successful-people-are-self-discipline-high-value-personal-management

Toleski, D., 'Best Parent Forward', *Australian Tennis Magazine* (2011)

REFERENCES

Wawrinka, S., Facebook, ATP Tour (2019) www.facebook.com/ATPTour/photos/its-never-a-sacrifice-when-you-love-what-youre-doingstan-wawrinka-mondaymotivati/10157496470803701

Williams, R., *Black and White: The Way I See It* (Atria Books, 2014)

Further Reading

Coyle, D., *The Talent Code: Greatness Isn't Born. It's Grown* (New York: Random House Publishing Group, 2009)

Djokovic, N., *Serve to Win: The 14-day Gluten-free Plan for Physical and Mental Excellence* (New York: Random House Publishing Group, 2013)

Giampaolo, F., *The Tennis Parent's Bible: Second Edition* (CreateSpace Independent Publishing Platform, 2016)

Gilbert, B., Jamieson, Steve, *Winning Ugly: Mental Warfare in Tennis – Lessons from a Master* (New York: Simon & Schuster, 1994)

Gladwell, M., *Outliers* (London: Penguin, 2009)

Ross, A., *Coaching Mentally Tough Tennis: Lessons from the Trenches* (California: CreateSpace Independent Publishing Platform, 2015)

Syed, M., *Bounce: The Myth of Talent and the Power of Practice* (New York: HarperCollins Publishers, 2010)

The Authors

Ryan Henry and Luke Bourgeois understand the elite player journey from first-hand experience.

Ryan started playing tennis at the age of four, won multiple Australian national titles, achieved a world number one junior ranking in doubles and competed in the Australian Open men's singles and doubles main draw at the age of eighteen.

Luke was number one in Australia as a junior, won the Junior Australian Open doubles title and competed on the ATP tour for twelve years. Luke was also coached by Tony Roche and travelled and trained with Roger Federer for three years.

Tennis has created some incredible life-enhancing opportunities for both Luke and Ryan, such as travelling the world, competing in the grand slams, creating many lifelong friends and the personal development that's acquired through striving to be world class.

While they both had really fulfilling tennis careers, there were a lot of lessons learned along the way and Ryan and Luke are passionate about helping set their students up for the best possible future.

They now run Voyager Tennis Academy in Sydney which specialises in the development of elite players. They have helped hundreds of nationally ranked players through the journey, many of whom have gone on to play college or professional tennis.

For more information please contact:

⊕ www.voyagertennis.com

Printed in Great Britain
by Amazon